P9-DIH-169

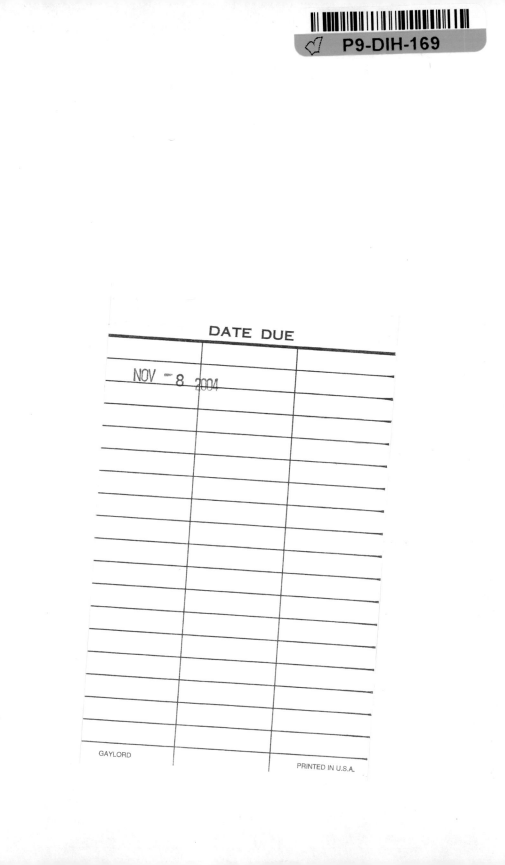

THE PRINCIPAL AS SCHOOL MANAGER

HOW TO ORDER THIS BOOK

BY PHONE: 800-233-9936 or 717-291-5609, 8AM–5PM Eastern Time

BY FAX: 717-295-4538

BY MAIL: Order Department
Technomic Publishing Company, Inc.
851 New Holland Avenue, Box 3535
Lancaster, PA 17604, U.S.A.

BY CREDIT CARD: American Express, VISA, MasterCard

THE PRINCIPAL AS SCHOOL MANAGER

William L. Sharp, Ph.D.
Southern Illinois University at Carbondale

James K. Walter, Ed.D.
Dudley Charlton (Massachusetts) Schools

LANCASTER · BASEL

The Principal as School Manager
a **TECHNOMIC**® publication

Published in the Western Hemisphere by
Technomic Publishing Company, Inc.
851 New Holland Avenue, Box 3535
Lancaster, Pennsylvania 17604 U.S.A.

Distributed in the Rest of the World by
Technomic Publishing AG
Missionsstrasse 44
CH-4055 Basel, Switzerland

Printed in the United States of America
10 9 8 7 6 5 4 3 2

Main entry under title:
The Principal as School Manager

A Technomic Publishing Company book
Bibliography: p.
Includes index p. 179

Library of Congress Catalog Card No. 94-60442
ISBN No. 1-56676-127-1

To the men and women who have the task of managing America's schools every day.

WLS

To Harry Maxwell McCool, my mentor.
I want you to know you are my hero;
you are the wind beneath my wings.

JKW

CONTENTS

PREFACE

The Principal As School Manager is intended for two groups of people: (1) as a supplemental textbook for graduate students taking a course in elementary principalship, secondary principalship, school finance, and school facilities, and (2) as a resource book for practicing school principals.

The emphases in today's university courses on the principalship are on areas such as instruction, curriculum, and evaluation. This is appropriate, since these are very important areas. However, there are areas which are important to the success of the principal, but which are not directly related to the instructional process, and which are often neglected in regular textbooks. These areas, which are the subject of this book, cover important roles for the principal, which occupy much of a principal's time, are visible to the community, and sometimes are the criteria upon which a principal may be judged, even though these roles should not be considered as important as instructional ones.

To give real examples from only two areas covered in this book: one of the authors was a school superintendent. He was once told by the wife of one of his school board members that there was one thing she wished the school would do – empty the outside trash baskets. The other author of this book was a principal in a school district where an administrator was dismissed because of problems with the school's extracurricular account funds. These two examples point out the need for adequate instruction in two areas: school finance and school facilities *at the principal level.* In traditional school finance courses, the emphasis is on topics needed by the superintendent – state formulas, tax levies, and state worksheets. The principal needs instruction in extracurricular fund accounting and fund-raising procedures. Likewise, school facilities courses usually emphasize the superintendent's need to work with architects, and the procedures for planning new buildings. Principals need to learn how to schedule custodians and how to maintain their buildings.

Since areas such as curriculum and instruction are important roles for the principal, it only makes sense to teach the principal to become efficient and effective in accomplishing some of the noninstructional roles, so that the majority of the principal's time can be devoted to those tasks which are directly related to the instructional process. That is the purpose of this book.

ACKNOWLEDGEMENTS

I would like to thank Dr. Joseph L. Eckenrode and Susan G. Farmer of Technomic Publishing Company for their helpful suggestions; my parents, William B. and Elizabeth Sharp for their many years of work in education and for their life-long support of my work; and, I would like to thank my wife, Helen, for her constantly encouraging me to write, and for her example as an excellent writer herself.

W. Sharp

I would like to thank Mrs. Gayle Delphia, my secretary and my very able typist, who made many excellent suggestions. I am forever in her debt. I also want to thank my two children, Zachary and Andrea, for allowing me to use their word processor, and for their patience when I was crabby. Finally, I want to thank my wife, Deborah, for her continual encouragement and boundless understanding. Now, she can have her dining room and breakfast room tables back.

J. Walter

CHAPTER 1

Introduction to the Principalship

INTRODUCTION

The school principal, whether elementary or secondary, is the single most important person to a school's success. A successful school must have a strong leader, and the principal is the one who must provide this leadership. Ron Edmonds (1979), in his classic study of inner-city schools, found that strong leadership was vital to a successful school.

There have been many studies involving effective principals and successful schools. Jwaideh (1984) found that effective principals established goals for their schools, supported innovation, and exhibited flexibility. Reilly (1984) concluded that effective principals stressed student achievement. This finding was echoed by Leithwood and Montgomery (1982).

While studies concerning effective principals often stressed instructional leadership, the managerial side of the principal's role was not ignored. Sweeney (1982) mentions that among the activities of an effective principal are such things as scheduling meetings and reducing classroom interruptions, while Leithwood and Montgomery mention that effective principals were efficient in selecting and delivering supplies and providing for space. While teachers felt that principals should concentrate on instructional tasks, principals reported that providing finances and caring for facilities were examples of tasks which were just as important to the successful school as instructional leadership (Baughman, 1976). The contention of this book is that a principal must be an instructional leader *and* an effective manager.

HISTORY OF THE PRINCIPALSHIP

Today's principal is the "quintessential middle manager" as described by Morris et al. (1984). These writers discuss how, in the formal hierarchy, principals take orders from the superintendent and other central office personnel on one side and relay these orders to department heads, teachers, and students on the other side. In addition, there are the political forces – some formal and some informal – such as school boards, parent organizations, advisory councils, unions, the courts, student protesters, minority activists, gangs, textbook vigilantes, and single-issue parent groups. And the modern principal is the person in the middle of all this.

This was not always the case. Although the school principal was the first educational administration position to evolve in the United States (Wood, Nicholson and Findley, 1985), it did not happen overnight. The early "school" in this country consisted of a teacher who traveled to various communities and taught children in homes. Children would gather at a house for a few hours of instruction, then the teacher would leave this group to instruct another group of pupils in another location.

As communities grew, there were enough children to warrant the construction of a school building, often simply a room or two. With only one or two teachers in the school, there was still little need of administrative help. Hiring and budgeting could be handled by the early school committees. Sometimes one member of this lay board had primary responsibility for these tasks. As schools increased in size and the number of teachers increased, a head teacher was sometimes appointed by those in charge of education – the school committees (still called by that name in some states), the school trustee, or the school board. While the head teacher had some administrative responsibilities, the primary responsibility was still to teach. Ensign (1923) described the early evolution as follows:

> Indeed, it appears that at the height of the development of the academy, about 1850, the average number of teachers per school was but two. So, here again, as in the English schools and in our own Latin grammar Schools, the relative need for administration was small, far overshadowed by the teaching function.
>
> In the academies that attained considerable size the school heads were known by varying titles, such as head master, rector, preceptor, provost and occasionally principal. At Phillips Andover, one of the truly great academies of New England, the official title of Eliphalet Pearson, the first head was preceptor, but in the records he is frequently referred to as principal Pearson; and in 1786 the title was so designated in the contract of the new principal. (p. 187)

As schools grew in size and complexity, the administrative duties became too much for the lay person to do on a part-time basis. Principals took over some of the tasks, and superintendents later took over other tasks. (It is generally recognized that the first superintendencies were in Buffalo, New York, and Louisville, Kentucky, in 1837.)

While the head teacher had minor responsibilities, such as seeing that the building was locked, unlocked, and properly heated, the principal assumed additional duties, such as scheduling classes, assigning students, and maintaining discipline in the school. In most cases, budgets were decided by the school trustees or by a superintendent. The curriculum of the early schools was very simple and traditional, and supervision of teachers was not a major assignment, as there were very few teachers in a building. In fact, there was not a large distinction between the principal/head teacher and the other teachers.

Most administrative duties of the early principals were clerical in nature—records, reports, school organization, and school equipment (Pierce, 1934, p. 211). According to Pierce, there were several factors which contributed to the development of the school principalship:

(1) The rapid growth of the cities in the last half of the 1800s, with the increase in the number of students
(2) The grading of schools
(3) The reorganization of schools and consolidation of departments under a single department head
(4) The establishment of the position of a head assistant to free the principal from teaching responsibilities

Kimbrough and Burkett (1990) state that "according to most accounts, the formal designation of a principal in Cincinnati was about the middle of the 19th century. Yet the position of school principal is primarily a 20th-century development and was concomitant with the great growth of pupil enrollments after 1900" (p. 3). Pierce (1934) says that the principal mainly dealt with clerical responsibilities prior to 1850. During the next fifty years, the responsibility of the principal shifted from records and reports to school organization and general school management. By 1900, the principal had become a manager of the school rather than a head teacher of the school. Some of the responsibilities of the emerging principal were detailed by Pierce (p. 211).

- the right to graduate students on the basis of the principal's standards

- the right to have orders to teachers given directly by the principal
- the right to have a voice in teacher transfers and assignments
- the right to enforce safety standards for students
- the right to supervise custodians and order supplies for the school

Bookbinder (1992) mentions the role of the superintendent with regard to the principal when he says, "The administrative duties of the principal were in place before the supervisory function was fully realized; as a result, the former has often tended to occupy the major portion of the principal's energies and efforts. Further, in many school systems, it was the superintendent who assumed the supervisory role and the improvement of instruction. This was his or her responsibility, if it was to be done at all" (p. 11). As schools grew and the responsibilities increased, the superintendent could no longer devote the time necessary to instructional supervision. Thus, the principal began to assume this additional role. By the early 1900s, principals were involved in the general organization and management of the schools, were in charge of supervision of instruction and staff development, and were charged with the responsibility of school/community relations (Pierce, 1934, p. 213).

The schools increased greatly in size in the 1950s and 1960s, causing new school buildings to be constructed all over the country. More principals were needed for these buildings, and the superintendents who may have been involved in supervision of instruction spent much of their time dealing with architects, contractors, and suppliers of school equipment. Principals, except those in very small schools, became full-time administrators with many and varied responsibilities. These responsibilities increased as special education and legal issues became prominent in the 1970s and 1980s. Some of the current duties of the principal, and some of the issues affecting them, are listed in Table 1.1.

With all the roles and responsibilities of the school principal, the person who assumes this position needs all the help and support he or she can get. This book is written to provide help with some of the managerial duties.

THE PURPOSE OF THIS BOOK

Roles and Responsibilities of the Principal

The authors feel that managerial responsibilities are a legitimate and important part of the overall role of the principal. While many of today's

Table 1.1. Duties of a Principal.

— curriculum development	— instructional supervision
— evaluation of teachers	— program evaluation
— writing of grants	— pupil transportation
— food service	— legal problems
— facility management	— budget development
— community relations	— technology in the school
— contract management	— union relations
— grievance responses	— assisting with negotiations
— supervision of other administrators	— guidance services
— supervision of athletics	— department heads
— student activities	— special education
— coordination with other district principals	— vocational education
— working with area principals	— working with central office
— recommending staff for hire	— health service
— directing secretaries and clerks	— discipline hearings
— student management	— student records
— due process hearings	— accountability
— student and staff scheduling	— decreased funding
— working with cooperatives in special education and vocational eduction	

textbooks stress the importance of the instructional role—and rightly so—they often omit, or give only cursory attention to, the managerial role. When this role is included, these textbooks sometimes look upon it from the superintendent's position rather than from that of the school principal. For example, a chapter on school finance might cover the state formula for equity in funding, and a chapter on facilities might cover working with the architect on constructing a new building. This book covers the managerial role, and it covers it from the principal's perspective.

Other authors have recognized that the principal has managerial responsibilities in addition to instructional ones. Knezevich (1975), while mentioning the instructional role, also says that the principal is "the school disciplinarian, the organizer of the schedule, . . . the manager of the school facilities, the supervisor of custodial and food service employees within the building . . ." (pp. 394–395). Lipham and Hoeh (1974) quote from an Illinois principal's job description and include, among other items, responsibilities for overseeing student conduct, fire, air raid, and tornado drills, school activities, noon lunch organization, collection of money from students, maintaining good public relations with the community, care of the building, grounds, furniture, and other property of the school, and requiring high standards of custodial services (pp. 122). Gorton and McIntyre (1978) report on a study by the National Association of Secondary School Principals which stated that principals need training in school-community relations and time management, as well as in the instructional role. Parkay and Hall (1992, pp. 28–29) conducted a study of principals which resulted in their textbook. When asked to rank their top internal issues, principals listed the following (the rank is shown):

- 2–establishing and improving channels of communication
- 6–establishing better standards of discipline
- 8–working with school finance
- 10–working with problems related to the school building

Curriculum was rated ninth.

When the same principals were asked to list the issues external to the school, the first concern was "creating a better image of the school." The authors of the text state, "Their [the principals] responses indicate that today's beginning principals *do* see themselves as providing leadership for their schools' curricular and instructional programs, but a staggering array of problems deter them from devoting continuing attention and energy to this task" (p. 38). It is hoped that the chapters which follow in this book will help principals to be able to accomplish their managerial tasks, and reduce the "staggering array of problems" so they can devote the attention and energy to the instruction which Parkay and Hall feel is necessary.

In the book by Morris et al. (1984) mentioned earlier, principals are compared with executives outside education. Unlike these executives, principals, to do the job right, must spend a large proportion of their time outside their offices. In the study done by Morris et al., principals spent about 50 percent of their time in their offices and 50 percent away from the offices, often in face-to-face contacts with teachers, students, and other staff members (p. 211). Part of this nonoffice time is consumed by looking at the facility, checking the cafeteria, working with custodians and grounds people, and talking with parents and community people. These authors seem to feel that there is a symbolic value in this movement of the principal around the building, showing the flag. The principal also serves as a managerial broker, negotiating order throughout the building.

Finally, these authors feel that the principals place themselves in spots where something is likely to happen, so that they can assume the responsibility of solving a potential problem (pp. 212–213).

Goldhammer et al. (1971, pp. 66–67) asked principals what problems they encountered in their jobs. The responses indicated that 35 percent had problems in the instructional program, 21 percent in finances and facilities, 14 percent in school-community relations, and 14 percent in pupil personnel. Other areas with lower percentages were also listed.

Finally, there is another study by the National Association of Secondary School Principals as detailed by Kimbrough and Burkett (1990). This study asked principals to rank how much time they spent in each area of responsibility, and then to rank how they would *like* to spend their time in each area. While program development was ranked first as the area in which the principals *wished* they could spend the most time, school management ranked first in actual time spent, followed by personnel, student activities, and student behavior as second, third, and fourth.

The Dual Roles of the Principal

Several writers have recognized that the principal has two roles, that of the instructional leader of the school and that of the manager of the school. Roe and Drake (1974), as mentioned in Blumberg and Greenfield (1980, p. 21), suggest that the role of the principal has a dual emphasis in managing the school and providing direct instructional leadership to the work of the school staff. Morris et al. (1984, p. 16) state that "although instructional leadership remains the central expectation of the principalship, the scope of the school-site management role has grown substantially over the years." Lipham (1964) says that there are two functions for the principal: leadership and management. These two functions are interdependent. He further states that principals cannot be effective leaders without performing these management functions. Kimbrough and Burkett (1990, p. 31) also say that principals may delegate some tasks, but they cannot delegate one function and keep the other, since these two functions are not so easily separated. And, regardless of whether any tasks are delegated, the principal is still accountable for both functions. Principals have to know enough about these responsibilities to train their assistants to do these tasks and to know whether they are done correctly and efficiently.

> While the duties and responsibilities have continued to grow and increase in complexity, the expectation that principals serve the twin functions of providing instructional leadership and managing school affairs had been rooted firmly in the minds of school superintendents and school board members by the early 1900s, particularly in America's larger cities. (Blumberg and Greenfield, 1980, p. 10)

Several studies have shown that administrators spend their time on tasks involving financial management, plant management, and personnel, instead of spending time on areas such as educational leadership, general planning, supervision, and curriculum development (NASSP, 1979, already cited; American Association of School Administrators, 1952; Gross and Herriott, 1965).

> While many principals might dream of being effective instructional leaders by enhancing the activities of teaching and learning in their schools, in reality, their experience is shaped by the press of administrative and managerial functions that mitigate against that dream becoming fact. (Blumberg and Greenfield, 1980, p. 24)

From the literature, it is evident that the following statements are true:

(1) Principals have two functions: instructional leadership and school management.
(2) These two functions are both important. Neither can be ignored.
(3) While some individual tasks within a function may be delegated, the entire function cannot be delegated.
(4) Although many principals would like to spend more time on the instructional function, they often find their time consumed by the managerial function.

As a result of these findings, the authors wrote this book to try to help principals do a more effective and efficient job of accomplishing the managerial function. The task of the effective principal is to integrate all of the obligations into his/her vision of what a school should be, and do all of the tasks well.

CHAPTERS OF THE BOOK

Chapter 2 deals with school finance for the principal, including accounting for school building funds, ticket sales, petty cash, and fund-raising.

Chapter 3 helps the principal with school facilities, discussing cleaning, maintenance, repairs, and the building walk-through.

Chapter 4 discusses the role of the principal in public relations, both inside the building and in the community.

Chapter 5 deals with the personnel role of the principal, including contract management.

Chapter 6 discusses areas of school law as they relate to the principal, including religion in the school and student rights.

Chapter 7 presents standards for the food service area, especially procedures dealing with safety and sanitation.

Chapter 8 deals with the issue of student discipline and the due process rights of students.

Chapter 9 details the role of the principal in pupil transportation.

Chapter 10 discusses scheduling at the high school, middle school, and elementary school levels.

These chapters are followed by three appendices on the topics of public relations, detention and school rules, and computer software.

REFERENCES

American Association of School Administrators. 1952. *The American School Superintendency.* Washington, D.C.

Baughman, M. J. 1976. "A Study of the Degree of Agreement Between Principals' and Teachers' Perceptions of the Principal's Functions and Behaviors," *Dissertations Abstracts International,* 36, 7974-A.

Blumberg, A. and W. Greenfield. 1980. *The Effective Principal: Perspectives on School Leadership.* Boston, MA: Allyn and Bacon, Inc.

Bookbinder, R., Jr. 1992. *The Principal: Leadership for the Effective and Productive School.* Springfield, IL: Charles C. Thomas, Publisher.

Edmunds, R. 1979. "Effective Schools for the Urban Poor," *Educational Leadership,* 37:15–24.

Ensign, F. C. 1923. "Evolution of the High School Principalship," *The School Review,* p. 31.

Goldhammer, K. et al. 1971. *Elementary Principals and Their Schools.* Eugene, OR: Center for Advanced Study of Educational Administration.

Gorton, R. A. and K. E. McIntyre. 1978. *The Senior High School Principalship, Volume II, The Effective Principal.* Reston, VA: National Association of Secondary School Principals.

Gross, N. C. and R. E. Herriott. 1965. *Staff Leadership in Public Schools: A Sociological Inquiry.* New York, NY: John Wiley.

Jwaideh, A. R. 1984. "The Principal as a Facilitator of Change," *Educational Horizons,* p. 63.

Kimbrough, R. B. and C. W. Burkett. 1990. *The Principalship: Concepts and Practices*. Englewood Cliffs, NJ: Prentice-Hall, Inc.

Knezevich, S. 1975. *Administration of Public Education*. New York: Harper and Row.

Leithwood, K. A. and D. J. Montgomery. "The Role of the Elementary School Principal in Program Improvement," *Review of Educational Research*, p. 52.

Lipham, J. M. 1964. "Leadership and Administration," *Behavioral Science and Educational Administration*, D. E. Griffith, ed., *The Sixty-Third Yearbook of the National Society for the Study of Education*, Chicago, IL: University of Chicago Press.

Lipham, J. M. and J. A. Hoeh. 1974. *The Principalship: Foundations and Functions*. New York, NY: Harper and Row.

Morris, V. C., R. L. Crowson, C. Porter-Gehrie and E. Hurwitz. 1984. *Principals in Action: The Reality of Managing Schools*. Columbus, OH: Charles E. Merrill Publishing Co.

National Association of Secondary School Administrators. 1979. "Summary Report of the Senior High School Principal," Vol. III, Reston, VA.

Parkay, F. W. and G. E. Hall. 1992. *Becoming a Principal*. Boston, MA: Allyn and Bacon, Inc.

Pierce, P. R. 1934. "The Origins and Development of the Public School Principalship," Ph.D. dissertation, The University of Chicago.

Reilly, D. H. 1984. "The Principalship: The Need for a New Approach," *Education*, 104.

Roe, W. H. and T. L. Drake. 1974. *The Principalship*. New York, NY: Macmillan.

Sweeney, J. 1982. "Principals Can Provide Instructional Leadership: It Takes Commitment," *Education*, p. 103.

Wood, C. L., E. W. Nicholson and D. G. Findlay. 1985. *The Secondary School Principal*. Boston, MA: Allyn and Bacon, Inc.

CHAPTER 2

School Finance for Principals

INTRODUCTION

This chapter discusses areas of school finance which affect the building principal. The first section comes from traditional school finance material and gives the principal a short course in the language used in school finance. Although most of the areas in this first section will not come up in the day-to-day operation of the school, a principal should know and understand these terms in order to work with the central office, and to intelligently discuss school finance with citizens. If you are a principal who has recently completed a good course in school finance, you may choose to skip this section and go right to the rest of the chapter. On the other hand, it might not hurt to review. The other sections of this chapter, including accounting for school funds, ticket sales, petty cash funds, fund raising, and budgeting, are topics which do affect the principal directly.

SEVEN THINGS PRINCIPALS SHOULD KNOW ABOUT SCHOOL FINANCE

1. Taxes Fund Schools

Since school districts, like other public institutions, have no sources of revenue (like profits from sales), they have been given the power to tax individuals and companies. This power comes from the state and is delegated, along with other powers, to local boards of education. At the local level, the most common tax used for school purposes is the *property tax*. It is a function of three variables: (a) the tax base, (b) the assessment practice used, and (c) the tax levy or rate.

The *tax base* consists of all the taxable property in the school district. Obviously, churches, state forest land, state hospitals, and other special areas are not taxable property. School districts which have a lot of acreage of this kind, and thus do not receive property taxes for these areas, may suffer from having a smaller tax base.

The *assessment practice* which is used varies from state to state, and sometimes may vary within a state. A state establishes some percentage which is applied against the market value of all property. The market value is the dollar amount a person would get for the property if it were to be sold. One state might multiply this market value by 35 percent (Ohio, for example) while another might choose 33 1/3 percent (most of Illinois, for example). Still another might assess property at 100 percent of the market value. Each state sets its own assessment practice.

The final variable is the *tax rate.* The school district's tax rate is multiplied by the assessed value of the tax base of the community to yield the amount of money the school will receive.

Here is an example, using one house. Assume that the market or sale value of a house is $90,000. If the assessment practice in the state is 35 percent, then the assessed value of the house would be $90,000 × .35 or $31,500. This is the amount upon which the homeowner would be taxed. If the tax rate is .08, then the taxes for the school district would be $31,500 × .08 or $2,520. If this concept is expanded to include all taxable houses, land, and businesses, then the school would receive the money resulting from a calculation using the whole tax base, not just this one house. It should also be remembered that a homeowner's tax rate includes taxes other than the school tax. Finally, the tax rate is expressed in different ways in different states (mills, dollars per hundred dollars of assessed valuation or per thousand dollars of assessed valuation, etc.).

2. Tax Exemptions

The above example is a simplified version of what actually happens. The state sometimes establishes various exemptions in order to give tax reductions to segments of the population. For example, there are sometimes reductions for people who live in the home they own (instead of renting it out to someone else who lives there), to veterans, to senior citizens, and to other groups. These exemptions either reduce the assessment of the home or reduce the tax by a fixed amount or percentage. In either case, less money arrives at the schoolhouse door. In addition, tax revenue may be reduced because some areas in the community have been given a tax break to encourage a business to expand or to move into the area. Every few years, someone (usually a county official) does a new appraisal of the area, taking into account such things as recent property sales and building permits, in order to arrive at a current value. At the same time, the school district may be changing its tax rate by action of the board of education and, possibly, by a vote of the citizens. Either change would alter the amount of revenue the school would receive.

3. Arguments against the Property Tax

Principals should understand some of the arguments against the property tax, since these often come up in discussions with members of the community, especially when talking with those who own a great deal of land, like farmers. First, the problems with the assessment process seem apparent: the assessment is subject to human error in judgement, to political changes due to exemptions, and to economic considerations when tax breaks are given to certain businesses. However, the main argument against the property tax is that it is no longer a fair measure of tax-paying ability. Years ago, the rich people put their money into land, so to tax people on the basis of the amount of land they owned seemed fair. Today, it is different. Rich people may put their money into land, but many put their money into the stock market, bonds, money market funds, mutual funds, and many other areas. Land is no longer the symbol of wealth. Yet, people are taxed at the local level on the value of the land they own, not on their wealth. Of course, we have many other taxes, but these usually do not go directly to the schools at the local level.

4. Funds per Pupil

Here are two terms a principal may hear: *cost per pupil* and *valuation per pupil.* Often, these are used to compare different school districts. It may be inappropriate to do so, but it is done. The cost per pupil is just that, the expenses of a school district during a school year divided by the number of students in the district. Here are two examples:

School District A	School District B
$ 5,000,000 expenditures	$ 6,000,000 expenditures
1,500 no. of pupils	2,000 no. of pupils
= $ 3,333.33 cost per pupil	= $ 3,000 cost per pupil

District A spends $5 million a year on 1,500 students, or about $3,333 for each student. District B spends about $6 million on its 2,000 students, or $3,000 per student. Note that, although District B spends more money in its budget than District A, it spends less on each student. Sometimes, this cost per pupil is considered to be a measure of educational quality.

Valuation per pupil is the assessed valuation of the district divided by the number of students. Consider another example with these districts:

School District A	School District B
$ 30,000,000 assess. val. of dist.	45,000,000 assess. val. of dist.
1,500 no. of pupils	2,000 no. of pupils
= $ 20,000 val. per pupil	= $ 22,500 val. per pupil

The assessed value behind each child in District A is $20,000 while the value behind each student in District B is $22,500. This factor, valuation per pupil, is sometimes considered a measure of taxable wealth of a district. Thus, in this example District B is wealthier than District A, yet its quality of education (at least as measured in the previous example) is less than District A because it spends less per student.

5. Equity in Education

Lately, cost and valuation per pupil calculations have led to discussions across the country about the concept of *equity.* Since there have been many legal cases concerning this issue, principals should have some background on this subject. The subject of equity (or fairness) comes from the concept that the quality of a child's education should not be based upon the wealth of the neighborhood in which he/she happens to live. The argument is that, within the same state, the state government has the responsibility to make sure that each child has an equivalent education, whether the child lives in a poor section of a city, a rich suburb, a farming community, or a very rural area. Obviously, the examples and calculations cited earlier show that the valuation of a district depends on the value of the homes and businesses in that district, and that certainly varies from place to place. While there are no simple solutions to this problem, most people feel that the state needs to become more involved in the funding of education, and to reduce the current reliance upon the local property tax.

6. Foundation Programs

Many states have a complex system of funding schools from the state level, and this short section on finance will not try to detail that system. However, principals should know about one aspect which is sometimes mentioned—the *state foundation program.* Sometimes called the state minimum, the practice means that the state sets a minimum (a foundation) of financial support for its schools. That is, the state guarantees (another term that is sometimes used) that each school will receive a certain dollar amount per student from a combination of local and state funds. The amount of state support may be affected by other factors in the state formula: the number of poor students, the education of the faculty, the amount of local financial effort, the number of special education and vocational students, etc. Each state which uses this system has different factors which it feels are appropriate to determine the amount of money a school district receives from the state.

7. The School Fund

The last term to be discussed is the school *fund.* A school fund is a self-balancing set of accounts established for a specific purpose. Although the school district may keep almost all its revenue in the same bank account, it keeps it separated into different funds with accounting practices. For example, the money used for teacher and administrator salaries, educational supplies and equipment, and fringe benefits is placed in one fund, often called the general fund or the educational fund. Other money is accounted for in a debt service fund in order to pay for the bond and interest payments on the buildings. Other funds which are self-explanatory might include a food service or cafeteria fund or a transportation fund. The actual names of the funds will vary from state to state, and local districts usually have the authority to establish other funds. Finally, the state regulates whether any money can be switched from one fund to another, and under what circumstances. In general, states tend to rule out such transfers, or at least make them difficult.

ACCOUNTING FOR SCHOOL BUILDING FUNDS

This section of the chapter is a practical, no-nonsense guide to help the school principal with the task of establishing and implementing procedures for money handling as it relates to the building level. Far too often, principals are given monetary responsibilities but are not given the necessary instructions to aid them in discharging these duties. School principals must be aware that the ultimate responsibility for fiscal matters in their schools rests upon them. Vigilance must be practiced at all times, since principals can be called upon to account for not only their actions but the actions of those they supervise.

While people reading this may say, "This problem could not occur in my school," or "I have to have some cash tucked away for emergencies," or "The people in my school are honest and wouldn't do anything to cause a problem," the reality is that fiscal problems do happen, even in schools with honest people who want to do the right thing. As a result, monetary mismanagement causes public criticism as well as problems with state accounting boards and, sometimes, local district attorneys who take a dim view of loose or improper accounting procedures.

Thus, it is important for the principal to take the responsibility to train teachers and staff in the importance of using proper accounting procedures for school funds. Brief in-service sessions during teachers' meetings and staff meetings should be used to emphasize the seriousness and the necessity of maintaining sound fiscal practices. Proper accounting practices are no longer a luxury, or something that pertains only to business; they must be a necessary and accepted part of the school operating procedures. The advice that follows results from the authors' administrative experience, not from legal credentials. It is always good advice to check with the school attorney or the state accounting agency for specific answers and procedures. Also, some states require specific forms for doing financial business. If that is not the case, feel free to use any forms printed in this book without seeking additional permission.

WHY DO FISCAL MANAGEMENT PROBLEMS EXIST IN SCHOOLS?

There is the assumption that all school people are honest and do not think about personal gain. While the overwhelming number of staff members are certainly honest, there are a few who will take advantage of a situation if the school does not have appropriate safeguards in place. Also, many honest school employees do not have any background in accounting, yet are asked to serve as activity sponsors and coaches who may raise money or collect it for some purpose. Likewise, teachers, especially in the elementary grades, often have to collect money for a variety of activities: school lunches, pictures, field trips, book clubs, etc. While the few dishonest people may skim a few dollars from the collections, the honest ones may cause problems by keeping money in drawers, closets, or their own homes overnight, or by not keeping good records on the money they collect. Most of these problems can be prevented by deciding upon, then implementing, rules regarding sound fiscal management, along with a systematic method of checks and balances. Throughout the following guidelines are actual cases which briefly discuss situations at schools where the authors have worked. These situations demonstrate the necessity for proper procedures.

GUIDELINES FOR HANDLING SCHOOL FUNDS

Every school should have a set of written guidelines which outline rules and regulations for handling funds. These written guidelines may be generated by the school district's business office, may result from careful reading of the state accounting handbook (if one is available), or may come from the building principal. The principal should consult with the district business official (and the state accounting agency, if one exists) to be certain that the school is following state law and proper accounting procedures. These procedures should allow money to be collected and disbursed in a forthright, legal manner, and should allow the principal and the business officers (treasurer, etc.) to examine what has transpired. Below are some guidelines concerning the proper handling of school funds by the staff.

Money Collection and Orders

Never use personal checking accounts as depositories for monies collected at school. Book club money, funds collected to buy cheerleader uniforms, and money from cheese and candy sales should go through the school books, not into personal checking accounts. Money which is

Deposit Slip
Checks ______________________ $________
Cash ______________________ $________
Coin ______________________ $________
Fund Account ______________________
Reason for Activity ______________________
____
Sponsor for Activity ______________________
Signature ______________________ Date ________

Figure 2.1 *Deposit Slip.*

collected should be given to the designated school official (school treasurer, bookkeeper, or other name which this section will call the *treasurer*). The teacher or sponsor should count the money, fill in the necessary information on the deposit slip (shown in Figure 2.1), and give it to the treasurer. The treasurer should issue a receipt for those funds (a copy of the deposit slip can serve as a receipt) and write a check and voucher to the book club company, the uniform company, or the cheese and candy firm. A clearing (sometimes called a revolving) account should be set up by the treasurer for this specific purpose. (Also, see the section in this chapter on fund-raising.)

Figure 2.2 shows an example of a payment voucher for the school's extracurricular accounts.

Don't Use Personal Funds

Students and staff should not make cash purchases from personal funds and request reimbursement through the school or activity funds.

> *Actual case:* An elementary teacher purchased some paint to paint her classroom and submitted the bill to the office. She did not have any authorization for the purchase or for the painting. She was not reimbursed for her expenses, and the word got around the staff that permission was necessary.

This is a typical problem at many schools. Staff members should charge items after the purchase has been cleared by the principal, who checks to see that the account is solvent. A call to the store or business can be made by the principal or sponsor to approve the charge. A bill is

CONSOLIDATED SCHOOL CORPORATION

PAYMENT AUTHORIZATION VOUCHER
SCHOOL EXTRA-CURRICULAR ACCOUNT

PAID BY CHECK: DATE: ____________ 19____

NO. ____________ DATE __________ 19____ No.

PURCHASED FROM ______________________________

ADDRESS ______________________________

PURCHASED FOR ______________________________

DELIVERED TO ______________________________

INVOICE SENT TO ______________________________

TO THE DISBURSING OFFICER:

THE FOLLOWING EXPENSE IS INCURRED PAYABLE FROM THE SCHOOL EXTRACURRICULAR ACCOUNT AND CHARGEABLE TO THE

______________________________ FUND

NO PAYMENT TO MADE FOR THIS ORDER UNTIL THIS FORM IS PROPERLY FILED AND THE ITEMS HAVE BEEN RECEIVED

QUANTITY	Description	UNIT	PRICE	TOTAL
		TOTAL THIS ORDER		

PRICED O.K. ☐
ITEMS RECEIVED O.K.
EXCEPT AS NOTED ☐

SIGNED ______________________________
CLAIMANT

APPROVED FOR PAYMENT ______________________________
SPONSOR

DATE ____________ 19____

(SIGN AND RETURN WITH INVOICE)

***Figure 2.2** Payment Authorization Voucher.*

then sent to the treasurer for payment. Any purchase not made in accordance with these procedures will not be allowed, and will be the responsibility of the one who made the purchase.

Organizations Should Maintain Separate Account Books

Each club or organization in the school should maintain a treasurer's account book. This book is helpful in reconstructing an audit trail (which is discussed later). From time to time, the club treasurer should check the club book against the school treasurer's account book.

Use Purchase Orders

The purchase order and payment authorization voucher shown in Figure 2.2 is to be used when an order is made for delivery at a later date. This form is to be executed in full and signed by the person authorized to make purchases for the activity. Before the activity sponsor is permitted to use the purchase order form, the sponsor must contact the school treasurer to determine if there is sufficient balance in the activity's fund to make the payment upon receipt of the merchandise. While some purchase orders have numbers already printed on them, other school districts prefer to have the treasurer give the sponsor a purchase order number to write on the order when the sponsor checks with the treasurer about funds. This issuance of the order number is an acknowledgement by the treasurer that funds are available in that account. Usually the form has at least three copies: one to be sent to the vendor for the order, one to be retained by the sponsor, and one to be sent to the school treasurer to be filed as an obligation (or encumbrance) against the account. The treasurer can then encumber the amount of the order so that the account will reflect the fact that there is an outstanding obligation against that account.

When the shipment is made, the vendor returns the payment voucher with the company's invoice (the bill). When the teacher or sponsor receives the order, the teacher must check the shipment against the invoice and voucher to see if everything which was ordered was received.

Often a company will send part of an order and backorder that which is not available. The sponsor must verify to the treasurer that which was received and that which was not received. The school treasurer receives the verification from the sponsor and pays the appropriate amount, depending upon the shipment. Note that the voucher (Figure 2.2) has a place to write in the check number and the date when the payment was made by the treasurer. The club treasurer's account book should also reflect this payment.

Ticket Sales

A particular school activity which can cause problems, and which can occur in many areas of the school, concerns ticket sales. Whether the activity is athletics, dramatic productions, musical programs, or dances, the sponsor of the event must be responsible for the proper accounting of all tickets, and keep a record of the number of tickets obtained, the number of tickets sold, and the number returned to the office. The sponsor also needs to make a proper accounting of the cash received from the sale of the tickets by indicating to the school treasurer the beginning and ending ticket numbers on the deposit slip and on the ticket report (shown in Figure 2.3). All tickets should be purchased from an outside vendor and should be prenumbered. Do not ask the school print shop to print tickets.

At least two different colors should be purchased so that the principal can vary the use of tickets. If possible, tickets should be collected, although the logistics of some events may make this practice difficult. The beginning and ending ticket numbers will help to verify the cash collected, but the physical evidence of the original collected tickets simply adds one more layer of proof. After verification by more than one person, the tickets can be disposed of so they cannot be used again. Another safeguard to consider is to have one person selling tickets at one location and another person collecting tickets at a different location, providing an easy verification of monies collected and tickets used. The ticket report shown in Figure 2.3 can be used to show the beginning and ending ticket numbers, the names of persons selling and collecting tickets, and other expenses. Figure 2.4 gives additional instructions for the ticket report. The cautious administrator may want to staple a duplicate bank deposit slip to the ticket report and photocopy it.

Money collected from ticket sales should be delivered by the teacher, coach, or sponsor as soon as possible for bank deposit. No funds should be kept in classrooms, at home overnight, or in a car.

Actual case: A high school cheerleading sponsor took cash home overnight and stored it in cigar boxes. She said she was honest and could see

Activity ______________________ Sponsoring Organization ______________
Date ______________________ Sponsor ______________
Time ______________________ Complimentary Tickets ______________
Location ______________________ Ticket Color ______________

Strating Ticket #	Ending Ticket #	Tickets Sold	Price per Ticket	Total Sales	Verified
1______	______	______	______	______	______
2______	______	______	______	______	______
3______	______	______	______	______	______
4______	______	______	______	______	______
Total		______	______	______	______

Receipts # ______ Date of Deposit______ Amount ______ (1)
Total Long or Short ______

Deposited to following:
Fund or Funds
______________ Amount ______________
______________ Amount ______________
______________ Amount ______________
____
Total ______________ (1)

Expenses	Individual	Amount
Referee ______	______	______
______	______	______
______		______
______	______	______
	Total (2)	______

(1) Gross Income ______ (2) Expenses ______ = Net Profit ______

Sponsor ______________________________

Figure 2.3 Ticket Report.

This report is to be used by all sponsors conducting an activity where the purchase of a ticket is necessary for participation.

1. The activity line requires a brief description of the activity.
2. The date listed should be the date of the activity, not the date of the report.
3. The time and location refer to the activity.
4. The sponsoring organization listed should be the club or extracurricular organization conducting the activity.
5. Complimentary tickets—If any complimentary tickets are issued, list how many tickets were given out and a brief description of the reason. They must be numbered and a record kept of who received the tickets.
6. List ticket color.
7. All tickets issued for an activity should be prenumbered. Before any tickets are sold, the beginning ticket number should be recorded and verified by at least two people. At the end of the activity, the ending ticket number should be verified by at least two people. If tickets were sold at more than one location, this procedure should be followed for each location. The necessary computations should be made to arrive at total sales.
8. An official receipt should be obtained from the extracurricular treasurer for the amount of the deposit. The receipt and deposit information should then be recorded on this line and copies of the receipt and deposit slip attached to the ticket report.
9. If an activity's proceeds are to be divided between more than one fund, the division should be detailed on the report.
10. No extracurricular expenses are to be paid in cash.
11. All tickets reports should be signed by the sponsor.

Figure 2.4 *Instructions for Complete "Ticket Report."*

no reason why she could not keep the cash safe at home. She was replaced as sponsor.

The reason banks have night depositories is so that cash from activities such as these can be placed into the bank that night rather than taken home or deposited in the morning.

Don't Pay People in Cash

The school should never allow anyone working a school function to be paid in cash. This includes ticket takers, off-duty security police, disc jockeys, and referees.

Actual case: Supervisors of the high school dance took cash from students attending the dance and then divided up the money at the conclusion of the dance. The amount they made for each dance depended upon the attendance. They defended their practice by stating that low attendance resulted in low pay, and that they had had many dances where they did not get paid much. The sponsors were told that they would be paid a set amount in the future, regardless of attendance. All cash had to be turned into the school. They decided they did not want to supervise dances under these new conditions.

Checks should be made out for each person being paid, and the person receiving the check should sign for the check to prove that it was received.

Petty Cash Funds

Another confusing issue to some school employees is the concept of petty cash funds. While there is a legal and proper procedure for establishing such a fund, many schools have what they call a petty cash fund which is improperly established.

When schools take money from cash paid to the office for various small items, or from dances which did not use numbered ticket sales, or from other sources where money was skimmed off the top, this is called an unverified petty cash fund, a slush fund, or just a cash bag. This type of operation is an unrecorded funds operation and must be stopped immediately. There is no paper trail to show where the money came from, how much was obtained from what sources, or where the money went. There must be accountability for all fiscal transactions, and the above scenario does not have such accountability. Merely placing receipts in the bag or box telling what the money was spent for will not solve the problem. There still is no verification of the original amount or source. For example, if the receipts show that $55.37 has been spent from the cash box, we still do not know that someone did not take out $30 for themselves, as there is no official record of the original amount. To repeat—documents supporting expenditures are virtually worthless unless the school treasurer can show supporting evidence that monies were received and deposited. Cash bag operations, a widespread practice in the past, can place a principal in serious financial difficulty.

Actual case: A principal was hauled away from his office in handcuffs by the local police because they suspected he was involved in taking cash from the school. School records could not be found to verify where all the cash came from or where it went. Although a grand jury later found the principal innocent, his reputation was destroyed by the investigation, which found others in the school guilty.

Because there are reasons for a principal to make some purchases without a lot of paperwork (postage due or stamps, for example), a principal can establish a verifiable and school-district-approved petty cash fund. The establishment of such a petty cash fund is accomplished by issuing a separate check for that purpose. Petty cash funds should never contain a large amount of money, and most principals agree that fifty dollars is quite adequate. Whenever disbursements are made from the fund, receipts must be obtained. When the fund has been depleted, the principal can take the receipts to the school treasurer and obtain a check to replenish the fund. At the end of the district's fiscal year, any remaining petty cash should be receipted back into the fund from which it was drawn in order to be included in the annual financial report. No cash should be kept over into the new fiscal year. A new check should be issued in the new year.

Cash Change Boxes

Many events occur at schools that necessitate the use of cash boxes to make change for patrons who pay to see an athletic event or some other program where admission is charged. There is a procedure to follow, and it does not allow for the principal to reach into pocket or purse, nor does it allow the vending machine to be raided for the change.

The establishment of a cash change fund is accomplished by writing a check from the desired fund to the individual responsible for the cash change. The check should be noted with *cash change* written on the check. This check should be cashed at the bank, and proper change denominations should be obtained for use in the cash change box. When the program or event is finished, the cash change should be receipted back to the fund and a receipt issued to the person responsible for the cash change.

Checks

In most school activities, checks should be used whenever possible.

Actual case: The secretary in charge of scheduling bus drivers for athletic trips, extracurricular trips, and field trips paid the drivers in cash for these trips. The cash came from students who paid for the trips or from the athletic fund. When this practice was discovered, it was immediately halted and all drivers were paid by check. The drivers were upset because they felt this money was tax-free.

No transactions should be done in cash if they can be avoided. Certainly, there should be no cash disbursements except for those rare occurrences that are handled by the properly established petty cash fund. When possible, principals and treasurers should encourage school patrons to use checks rather than cash. Checks provide a permanent record that helps build good school financial practices and provides lasting visual proof that cash transactions simply cannot match.

Another safety factor can be added to the practice of using checks—require two signatures on each check issued by the school. No one person should have the authority to write and sign checks or to withdraw funds from bank accounts. Personal integrity is a valuable attribute, and requiring two signatures is an ideal safeguard for avoiding problems and protecting the reputation of those involved in handling money. For school expenditures, the school administrator and the treasurer or bookkeeper can be the two cosigners. For club accounts, a third signature can be added—the sponsor of the club. In this way, the club sponsor cannot accuse the principal of unilaterally deciding to use club funds for another purpose. This third signature functions as a courtesy to the sponsor, and also diminishes the pressure placed on the principal by allowing a shared responsibility for the expenditures from the account. It is normal practice to have the two school cosigners (principal and treasurer) sign signature cards which are kept on file. A third person (assistant principal, assistant bookkeeper, etc.) is sometimes asked to sign such a card and will serve as cosigner only in the absence and approval of the principal.

Bonding

One of the best things a school district can do for its employees who handle money is to establish a blanket bond or a fidelity bond. This will allow an institution, the bonding company, to accept the liability for funds taken by dishonest personnel. It then becomes the bonding company's responsibility to make certain that dishonest personnel pay for their indiscretion. The process of bonding employees is relatively inexpensive, and it should certainly be considered by the school district as a necessary safeguard for those persons who handle money. Principals also need to be bonded to make them more responsive to supervision of any treasurers in their buildings. Some states have treasurers in each building; others only in the central office. State laws usually require that the district treasurer or bookkeeper be bonded, so that should have already been done.

Bank Deposits

A problem, and potentially a major scandal, that seems to plague many schools is the practice of infrequent visits to the bank to make deposits. Both principals and treasurers acknowledge that they should go to the bank with a deposit, but something always seems to occur to force them to put it off to another day. Deposits should be made daily, if at all possible. Funds should not be kept at school overnight. Night depositories should be used if the official cannot get to the bank during banking hours. It is a good practice for the treasurer to make a daily routine of making deposits at the bank at the end of the workday. As stated earlier, these night depositories should be used by school personnel after night activities. No money should be taken home. If the school has a large amount of money coming in a certain day (like registration day), the person in charge should make several deposits throughout the day and not keep a large amount of money at the school all day. Again, the school should encourage the use of checks rather than cash on days like this.

Fund-Raising

With today's financial crunch, more and more schools are turning to product sales or fund-raisers to help defray the costs of items that school district budgets never seem to provide. Many of these fund-raisers generate thousands of dollars in both gross and net profits.

Whenever possible, it is best for a nonschool organization like the PTA, PTO, booster club, etc., to raise the money and then present the school with a check, or with the actual supplies or equipment needed. When this is done, the principal has no responsibility for receiving cash or accounting for it. The organization has that responsibility. However, as ideal as this is, most schools find themselves involved in fund-raising, and thus accountable for the cash received.

Once again, the school personnel must be extremely cautious, since

PRODUCT SALES REPORT

(A copy of this report must be given to school treasurer with deposit)

Activity ____________________ Sponsor ____________________

Sponsoring Organization ____________________

SALES

Total units purchased ________ Cost per unit ____________

Less units remaining after sales complete* ________ *Verified by ____________ (vendor or sales representative)

TOTAL UNITS SOLD ________

Selling price per unit ________

TOTAL SALES ____________

Less total cost ____________

RECEIPTS AND DEPOSITS

Profit ____________

Receipt Number	Date	Date of Deposit	Amount

TOTAL RECEIPTS AND DEPOSITS ____________

CASH (SHORT) OR LONG ____________

Fund or Account	Amount Deposited	Date Deposited

How was inventory unsold disposed of at the end of the sales project?

____

____

Sponsor

***Figure 2.5** Product Sales Report.*

cash is often used rather than checks. In order to bring more accountability into fund-raising activities, a product sales report may be used (Figure 2.5).

Note that the report has a space for total units purchased. This means the total units invoiced and paid for, or the total units obtained on consignment–which can be returned to the vendor. The report has a place for cost per unit as well as a place to figure the profit. There is also a section for receipts and deposits which allows for monies to be turned in and deposited. Each receipt and deposit can then be verified by both the sponsor and treasurer. Instructions for completing the product sales report are given in Figure 2.6.

This report should be used by all sponsors conducting any activity where there will be products or merchandise for sale.

1. Activity—description of the activity or product being sold.
2. Sponsoring organization—the organization or club sponsoring the activity.
3. Sponsor—the teacher or person in charge of and responsible for inventory and receipts.
4. Total units purchased—this should equal the total units invoiced and paid for. If any units were sold on consignment, any units remaining after sales will be returned to the vendor. In this case, the total units purchased will equal total units sold and the units invoiced and paid for. If an activity is on a per order basis, there will not be any units remaining after sales. In that case, the total units purchased and sold will be the same.
5. Less units remaining after sales complete—if applicable, any units that were not sold. An explanation should be made of how the inventory was disposed of (returned to vendor, used for prizes, etc.).
6. Total units sold—total units purchased less units remaining after sales complete.
7. Selling price per unit—if there are items with different unit selling prices, a product sales report will need to be completed for each item having a different unit price. If this is the case, a summary report should be made detailing total receipts and deposits.
8. Total sales—selling price unit times total units sold.
9. Less total cost—of the entire product from distributor or supplier.
10. Profit—retail price of total sales less total cost from distributor or supplier.
11. Receipts and deposits—this is the money received which should be given to the school extracurricular treasurer, and an official receipt obtained for the amount given to the treasurer. This receipt information should then be recorded in this section, with the date of deposit completed by the school treasurer.
12. If any activity proceeds are to be divided between more than one fund, the division should be shown here along with date(s) of deposit.
13. All product sales reports must be signed by the sponsor.

***Figure 2.6** Instructions for Product Sales Report.*

Request to Raise Funds

Date__________

The ____________________(club or organization) wishes to have a fund-raising activity on ________________(date) until ______________, 19___. There will be __________(number of) students participating. The nature of the fund-raising activity will be____

____

Fund-raising materials will be supplied by ______________

_____________________________(name of company)

we expect to earn $________ profit for the following purpose

____

Sponsor________________________________

Decision of Principal: Approved ________Denied__________

Principal_______________________________

Figure 2.7 Request to Raise Funds.

The deposit slip shown in Figure 2.1 can be used to deposit funds received. A copy of the form should be kept in the sponsor's club or activity records to verify monies deposited.

One of the problems with fund-raising has nothing to do with fiscal matters but will be mentioned here anyway. Sometimes clubs go overboard with fund-raising, spending most of their time raising funds and forgetting the original purpose of the club. Also, organizations and clubs can be given a sales pitch by the same person every year and end up selling the same thing to the same community. There is a limit to the amount of cheese and candles students can sell in one year. To prevent these problems, the principal needs to have a way to control fund-raising. Figure 2.7 shows a request to raise funds which can be used by the principal to control what is occurring in the building and the community.

Audits

Although many administrators are gregarious and enjoy meeting people and answering questions about their school, there is a dichotomy which occurs whenever someone suggests that the principal open the school books for an audit. Some principals become quite upset that any outsider would dare to question fiscal matters in the school.

This attitude is absurd, and is quite dangerous for any principal to assume. Openness is the finest form of protection and honesty that a building principal can employ. Principals should, in fact, welcome an audit, since audits allow the principal to become more aware and more in control of the fiscal management within the school. The auditor, whether from an accounting firm or from a state accounting office, can recommend and clarify items or problems that have arisen during the school year. Auditors should be viewed as agents who want to help schools operate smoothly within a legal framework and according to accepted accounting principles.

Audits are especially helpful to newly appointed principals who can use the audit to change any questionable (or downright illegal) practices that their predecessors may have used in fiscal management. The wise principal will ask for an audit upon appointment to a new position to see that all procedures are examined by an outside agent. Also, the auditor can ask the bookkeeper or treasurer to explain the procedures and rationale for what has been occurring with regard to fiscal matters, and can relieve the principal of having to challenge the treasurer in his/her first weeks on the job.

In addition to external audits by state agencies or accounting firms, the school district may want to hold periodic internal audits. This can be accomplished by having one fiscal officer of the district check the procedures which are being followed by the bookkeeper in a particular school. This internal audit has the advantage of an additional audit check at no cost to the district.

It is imperative that school principals maintain a good audit trail. Principals need to communicate regularly with the treasurer and be sure that financial records of their school reflect careful attention to detail. They should maintain accurate and systematic records so that an auditor can simply look at the written record to reconstruct financial transactions. Below are some general guidelines to help develop a proper audit trail, and to serve as a summary of the main points of this section of the chapter.

- Whenever there is any doubt as to why something was handled in a particular manner, jot down a brief explanation of the details.
- Use a pencil to total the columns on the ledger.
- Make certain that all records are both neat and legible.
- Always examine the amounts on receipts and checks.
- Always make certain that checks are supported by legitimate invoices.
- Always void checks or receipts in error and attach them to the duplicate.

- Always leave the receipt and check books in book form.
- Canceled checks and bank statements should be maintained together.
- Always circle and note anything unusual on the bank statements, such as bad checks, the redeposit of bad checks, or errors made by the bank or in the book.
- Always reconcile the monthly bank statement on receipt, rather than letting it go undone for several weeks or months.
- Receipts should always be issued whenever money is given to the treasurer.
- Receipts should always have either a person or an organization listed on the "Received of" line.
- A check should never be issued to "Cash."
- Checks and purchase orders should never be signed until they are completely filled out.
- Signature stamps should not be used, since the volume in the school would not be excessive.
- Receipts should be deposited, intact, as quickly as possible. Personal checks should never be cashed from this money prior to deposit so that a clear audit trail can be maintained.
- It is necessary to inform the treasurer and the staff that no personal checks will be cashed. Doing this may be unpopular with the staff, but it will save a tremendous amount of headaches.
- Do not deal in cash. Deposit monies from vending machines or the bookstore as quickly as possible.
- Use a night depository. Do not leave cash in the building overnight.
- Do not pay bills in cash, even if you have a receipt to prove legitimacy.
- Do not allow unrecorded funds in your building. This includes coffee funds, library fines, or any other type of slush funds or cash bag operations. (Think of them as booby traps waiting to explode next to the principal.)

BUDGETING AT THE SCHOOL LEVEL

The role of the principal in the budget process will vary from district to district. The typical principal makes some recommendations to the superintendent (or other central office administrator) and later receives a list of the budgets under the principal's control and the amount approved for each budget. One exception to this is the principal, often in a large district, who has no budgetary responsibilities, with each teacher being given a budget which can be used to order supplies from the district inventory. Another exception is the principal who is given a great deal of budget responsibilities, such as in site-based budgeting. This latter exception will be discussed at the end of this section.

There are several systems of budgeting which can be used at either the district or school level. In most cases, these are employed at the district level by the business official and the superintendent. However, it is possible that they could be used at the school leave, or that principals will be involved in the district-level budgeting. Thus, these systems are discussed in this chapter in finance.

Program Budgeting

PPBS, which stands for Planning, Programming, Budgeting System, involves the following steps:

- The school (or district) establishes its goals for the year(s). These goals may be educational (to improve reading), involve personnel decisions (to hire minority teachers), relate to curriculum (to develop a new science program), or even involve the budget itself (to reduce expenditures by 10 percent). The goals may be set by a committee, by the board, by the teachers in a school, or any way the district agrees to do it.
- Once the goals have been established, the school determines different alternatives to reach those goals. For example, if the goal is to improve reading in the elementary school, the alternatives may involve a new reading program, new staff, in-service training, more supplies, special books, an expanded library, more librarian time, or any number and combination of alternatives.
- Next, the cost of each alternative is determined. This requires some research, some estimating of salaries, and some exploring of catalogs in the situation described above.
- Finally, a decision is made on the best alternative, looking at the

overall goals and objectives, the alternatives presented, and the costs of those alternatives.

The advantage of this budgeting system is that it spends money in relation to some agreed-upon goals. It makes spending more defensible. On the other hand, it does take time to go through this process.

Zero-Based Budgeting

In this budgeting system, each program has to be justified. It starts by having each program director describe the current program, and tell what progress was made during the past year. For example, at a high school, each department chair, athletic director, music director, health center nurse, etc., would be a "director."

- Having accumulated information about the past year, the directors would establish three recommended levels of funding for the next year. One level would be a *maintenance level* which would describe how the program would look and function if the funding level was the same for the next year. The second level is the *enhancement level* which would involve additional funding, if approved. In some districts, the administrator will set the amount (e.g., a 10 percent increase). In others, the directors are allowed to set the amounts themselves. Again, the directors explain what changes would be made in next year's program to account for this increase in funding. The third level of spending is a *reduction* from the current level. Again, it may be a set amount (10 percent for everyone), or it may be established by the individuals directors, keeping in mind that it is more difficult to let people elect their own reductions than it is to allow them to select their own enhancements. Each director submits all three levels of spending—maintenance, enhancement, and reduction—along with the programs, personnel, etc., for each, to his/her supervisor, probably the principal.
- The principal studies all levels, and ranks the levels/programs. The principal's rankings may then go to a central administrator, such as the superintendent, for further review and ranking. For example, the principal might select reading enhancement first, followed by mathematics maintenance, etc. Figure 2.8 shows

Input from Directors:

Reading Enhancement (R_E) Mathematics (M_E) Science (S_E) Ind. Arts (I_E)

Reading Maintenance (R_M) Mathematics (M_M) Science (S_M) Ind. Arts (I_M)

Reading Reduction (R_R) Mathematics (M_R) Science (S_R) Ind. Arts (I_R)

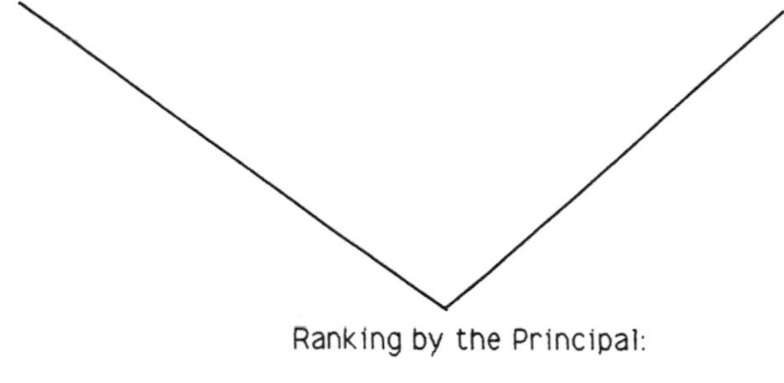

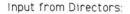

Ranking by the Principal:

1. R_E
2. M_E
3. S_M
4. I_R

These rankings would then be sent to the superintendent with the rankings from the other building principals so that a final ranking could be made.

***Figure 2.8** Example of Zero-Based Budgeting.*

how this might look. The superintendent might then select from the choices that arrive from all buildings.

While zero-based budgeting has the advantage of involving much of the staff in the budgetary process, it also consumes a great deal of time. Also, those areas which get reduced by this process will certainly think it was a waste of time and may feel that the person responsible for that area did not represent them well in the process.

Line-Item Budget

The line-item budget is important for two reasons. First, it is the most commonly used budgeting system, and second, all of the other systems end up in a line-item display.

- The administrator looks at last year's budget, line item by line item, and decides whether each item should be reduced, increased, or remain the same. This process can be done by the administrator working alone, with the help of others, or by using one of the systems of budgeting already mentioned. For each item, the following information is typically given: the name of the budget, the budget for this year, the budget for the last two or three years, the recommended budget for next year, and any rationale for a major change. Figure 2.9 shows how part of this budget would look. This system has the advantage of being

Description	2 Yrs. Ago	Last Yr.	This Yr.	Next Yr.	Comments
Field trips	950.00	875.00	800.00	800.00	Donated Fund
Office supplies	845.00	835.00	800.00	750.00	
Travel	450.00	375.00	375.00	375.00	
Contractual services	875.00	875.00	875.00	0	Discontinue
Equipment—new	400.00	300.00	250.00	300.00	See listing
Equipment—repair	250.00	250.00	200.00	200.00	
Consultants etc.	150.00	150.00	150.00	0	Not used

Figure 2.9 *Example of a Line-Item Budget.*

the simplest, and one which can easily be compared with other schools and districts. The disadvantage is that it may not be based upon any goals and may not involve anyone but the person making the recommendations.

School Site Budgeting (Unit Budgeting)

In school site budgeting, the decision-making responsibility is shifted from the central office to the school level, and that means the principal. Very few districts engage in a pure school site budgeting program. Some use a modified version. In a pure system, the central office would calculate the amount of money the school spends on all its budgets—personnel, utilities and buildings, supplies, equipment, etc. The principal would be told that he/she is responsible for budgeting for the next year for all these areas. Thus, the principal can shift funds from one area to another, eliminate an area, or expand another area. For example, the principal could decide not to purchase any new tables and desks, eliminate a secretary, and hire some new teacher aides for the building—or do the reverse. The principal may also decide to involve the staff a great deal in making these decisions or the principal may make them without their aid. (School staff involvement in decision making is discussed in detail in Chapter 4.)

The advantage behind this system is that the financial decisions are made where the programs are taking place. Since the principal has the responsibility for running the building, maintaining it, supervising it, and supervising all of the staff and programs, he/she should have the financial authority to accompany that responsibility. One disadvantage is the amount of time a principal would have to devote to the budget. Most principals do not have any extra time. Also, some principals would not have the desire nor the background to be in charge of such a budget. Many would fear that it would detract from the supervision of staff, development of curriculum, evaluation of teachers, and the opportunity to meet with students and parents.

As a result, many districts use a modified version of site-based budgeting by sending the principal the amount of money available for all supplies and equipment and letting the principal send back a budget detailing how this money should be divided up. Budgeting for personnel, utilities, transportation, etc., would be done at the central office.

SUMMARY

This chapter presented a short review of school finance, then discussed areas of accounting at the school building level, including ticket sales, petty cash funds, fund-raising, and budgeting. The next chapter discusses the principal's role in maintaining the school facility.

THE PRINCIPAL'S CASEBOOK

The Case of the Red Room

Arriving back from a short summer vacation, you notice that one of your classrooms has been painted a bright color. You did not authorize it, so you went to the custodian to ask why it was painted. The custodian said he did not know anything about it either. In going through your mail, you find a note from the superintendent: "I just got a bill for several gallons of paint from Mrs. Watson [second grade teacher]. Someone said they saw her painting her room. I did not authorize this expenditure. Did you?"

Questions to Consider

- What do you tell the superintendent? Do you cover for the teacher?
- Do you contact the teacher first or the superintendent?
- Not only did Mrs. Watson purchase something without any authorization, she also painted a whole room without any approval. How should you handle this situation with her?
- What can you tell the other teachers so that this is not repeated?

CHAPTER 3

The School Facility

INTRODUCTION

Many schools have been neglected over the past few years. As school budgets have tightened, major repairs have been eliminated or postponed, and minor ones, if done at all, have been done as cheaply as possible by custodial crews which have also been reduced for budgetary reasons. As a result, the routine of daily and periodic cleaning and maintenance is more important than ever. Because the principal is given the responsibility of supervising the maintenance of the school building, this chapter will provide suggestions in the areas of cleaning, maintenance, avoidance of hazards, and preventive maintenance. In addition, it will discuss the building walk-through, how to project classroom needs, an emergency plan, and the use of computers for maintaining facility records.

CLEANING

Cleaning, as used in this chapter, means the *daily* routine for custodians who sweep classrooms and halls, empty wastebaskets, dust tables and clean chalk boards, and do other similar duties. The next section of the chapter will discuss maintenance, which not only implies repairs but also is used to mean maintenance of the building itself by periodic (not daily) cleaning.

While some school districts contract out custodial services because they feel they may save money, or that they may lack the expertise to properly supervise the cleaning and maintenance of buildings, others feel it is important to have workers who are employed by the school. In these cases, the principal assumes the responsibility for the supervision of the custodians.

The school building principal needs to begin each school year by meeting with the custodians and discussing what their responsibilities are for the year. While some responsibilities will remain the same from year to year, the principal should evaluate the situation each year and decide if there should be a shift in who does what, when, and how. At this meeting, the custodians should be given a schedule which tells each of them what is to be done in their areas and when it is to be done. Figure 3.1 shows an example of a possible schedule for a custodian. Note that it is not extremely detailed. It simply tells the tasks to be done and when they should be done. Detailed information on some tasks will be given later in this chapter.

When planning custodian schedules and discussing their responsibilities with them, remember that schools are no longer used just by school people. Many community groups are not only allowed to use school facilities, they are encouraged to do so. As a result, custodians will often have to open up outside doors to the buildings in the evenings or weekends for these groups, open up doors to specific areas within the

7:00 – 8:00 AM	Open building, check results of night staff cleaning, fill out boiler room checklist, raise flag, check bld. for repairs while making rounds, check exit and hall lights for possible replacement, replace lunch room trash bags.
8:00 – 8:15 AM	Look at list left by principal for any specific instructions. Check locker area. Check bathrooms and flush where needed.
8:15 – 8:30 AM	Get frozen food out of freezer for cooks.
8:50 AM	Check locker rooms and bathrooms.
9:00 AM	Repair and maintain building according to cleaning and maintenance schedule posted in office.
9:30 AM	Check locker rooms and bathrooms. Continue to clean and make repairs, checking locker rooms and bathrooms every 30 – 45 minutes.
12:00 – 12:30	Lunch break. Continue with cleaning, repairs, and checks of locker rooms and bathrooms.
1:15 – 2:15 PM	Wash and stack tables and chairs in cafeteria. Dust off floors and empty rubbish cans.
2:15 – 2:30 PM	Break
2:30 – 3:15 PM	Check bathrooms and locker rooms, sweep where needed, clean drinking fountains.
3:15 – 3:30 PM	Discuss building maintenance and cleaning with night custodian. Report to principal for any last minute assignments.

Special assignments: In winter, check heating equipment to see if it is functioning correctly upon arrival at school. If there is snow, clear sidewalks and steps around building. If there is rain or snow, put out rugs at doors and get out buckets and mops for later use.

Figure 3.1 *Schedule for Day Custodian.*

buildings, give directions to areas, or directions on how to use some school equipment, locate the equipment and supplies for people, answer questions, clean up after the groups, etc. The attitude of the custodian could easily be, "I spend so much time doing things for these people, I can't get to my own job." While these activities will, on occasion, keep a custodian from doing part of the evening cleaning, or cause interruptions in the cleaning procedures, he/she does need to realize that these activities are a part of the job, not interference with the job. These groups are almost always composed of local citizens who are taxpayers and voters whose opinion of the school may be formed by the services offered to them (not to students) and the way they are treated at the school. The principal's public relations program cannot end when the students leave in the afternoon.

One of the purposes of this principal-custodian meeting is to discuss situations like the use of the building by outside groups and how that use affects so many things: the custodians' cleaning schedule, the attitudes of the adults using the building, and the support of the school's mission in general.

Another topic to discuss during this meeting is the overall work load of the custodians. The principal needs to discuss the specific jobs of the custodian and give them a list of these jobs, detailing how long each should take. These lists, sometimes called time standards, are available in books dealing with custodian work loads. An example is given in Figure 3.2. However, the principal should be aware of several things:

- These numbers usually do not include the preparation time, the time needed to get the supplies and materials ready, and to get to the location.
- These numbers are approximate, and do not allow for conditions which may be different in your building. Keep that in mind and change the numbers to meet local conditions. Experience from past years should be used to modify your time standards.
- Do not present these standards to the custodians without discussion, without getting their input from past experiences in your building.

Custodians would resent a principal giving them a generic list of time standards, without discussing it, and telling them that they are expected to meet these standards. The purpose of these standards should be to give both custodians and the supervising principal some idea of how long it should take to do a specific task. Obviously, the principal needs to adapt

Custodial Work	Frequency	Time Standard*
Classroom		
Dusting	Daily	5 min. per room
Sweeping	Daily	12 min. per room
Damp mopping	As needed	23 min. per room
Polishing	As needed	15 min. per room
Servicing classroom	Daily	15 min. per room
Removing waste paper, sweeping floor, dusting chalk tray and window sills, closing windows, adjusting temp. controls, noting needed repairs		
Servicing lavatory	Daily	35 min. per lavatory
Cleaning lavatory	Daily	1 min. per fixture
Cleaning toilet	Daily	1 min. per fixture
Cleaning urinals	Daily	2 min. per fixture
Cleaning urinal trap	Weekly	2 min. per fixture
Cleaning sink	Daily	2 min. per fixture
Mopping floor	Daily	2 min. per 100 sq. ft.
Stairways		
Damp mopping	Weekly	4 min. per flight
Sweeping	Twice daily	6 min. per flight
Other areas		
Cleaning drinking fountains	Daily	1 min. per fixture
Dusting fluorescent tubes	Monthly	12 tubes per min.
Sweeping auditorium	Daily	15 min. per 1,000 sq. ft.
Sweeping corridors	Twice daily	8 min. per 1,000 sq. ft.
Sweeping gym floor	Daily	5 min. per 1,000 sq. ft.
Washing glass	As needed	1 min. per 10 sq. ft.

*Time standards do not include preparation time or cleanup time following the completion of the work. Although local conditions may cause these times to vary, the above times are considered industry time standards and are useful guidelines.

Figure 3.2 *Time Standards for Custodians.*

these to the building and to allow a certain tolerance in enforcing the standards.

The PR and goodwill discussed earlier between custodians and the community groups are not the only good relations needed. The principal needs to remember internal relations as well as external relations. While this topic will be discussed in more detail in another chapter, it is appropriate to mention a few suggestions about custodians:

(1) The principal needs to emphasize to the custodians that they are important to the overall functioning of the school, and needs to find ways to show that this is true. When the principal discovers, during

his/her inspections, that the building is especially clean or that some special task was completed very well, the principal needs to remember to thank the custodians and mention that the job was done well. A written memorandum or a certificate of appreciation will be highly prized. Everyone who does a good job likes to know that someone noticed it.

(2) The principal should emphasize to the faculty and students that they can help custodians do their jobs by cooperating with them, by picking up papers, putting chairs on tables/desks (if that is the procedure), etc. This behavior should become second nature to students.

(3) Besides helping the custodians, the staff and students should treat the custodians well. This should go without saying, but sometimes the principal needs to remind others about this. The staff can compliment the custodians when appropriate, simply speak to them occasionally, and let them know that they are a part of the school, an important part. (Remember when you were a beginning teacher and another teacher told you to get to know John, the custodian, as he could help you a great deal? Still a good idea.)

(4) Finally, the principal should find ways to include the custodians (as well as other staff members) in the school activities from time to time.

MAINTENANCE

The second aspect of the custodian's responsibility is building maintenance, including periodic cleaning. While the custodian has certain daily cleaning duties such as cleaning all classrooms, halls, restrooms, emptying wastebaskets, etc., there are some duties which are done on an as-needed basis or on a scheduled periodic basis. Again, the principal needs to have these listed in writing for the custodians. In fact, it is probably more important to have these tasks than the daily tasks given to the custodians in written form because they are not done each day and can be forgotten.

REPAIRS AND MAINTENANCE

The principal needs to establish some procedure for people in the school to report repairs which need to be made, the assignment of those

Building: A R D B T W Other ______________ Room/Location ______________

To ______________ Requestor ______________ Date ______________

Work Priority: ☐ Emergency ☐ This Week ☐ No Rush ☐ Summer ☐ On/By

Work Description: ☐ Repair/Replace ☐ New Work ☐ Grounds ☐ Move ☐ Opinion ☐ Other ______________

____

____

Assigned to ______________ By ______________ Date ______________

Maintenance Use

☐ Needs Outside Contractor	☐ Needs Replacement	☐ Needs Parts	☐ Work
☐ Called	☐ Ordered	☐ Ordered	☐ Scheduled for ____
☐ Awaiting Approval	☐ In Stock	☐ In Stock	☐ Completed on ____
☐ On Hold	☐ Replacement on Hold	☐ On Hold	☐ Not Approved

Comments: ______________

____

____

Assigned to ______________ By ______________ Date ______________

BUSINESS OFFICE

Figure 3.3 *Maintenance/Custodial Work Request.*

repairs to a custodian, and a schedule to complete them. Figure 3.3 is an example of a form which can be used by staff to report something in need of repair. Note that it also can be used by the principal to assign that repair to a custodian. The principal keeps track of these assignments to be sure they are completed.

Some of the repair tasks might be:

- replacing lighting in classrooms and hallways
- replacing broken windows, doors, and locks
- repairing student lockers
- repairing fixtures and faucets in restrooms
- repairing/replacing pencil sharpeners
- repairing classroom desks, tables, playground equipment
- painting small areas which were damaged
- fixing leaks and repairing water fountains

Note that some of these are repairs which could have been submitted by someone in the school (e.g., The pencil sharpener in room 201 is broken.). On the other hand, there are some items which can be noticed by the custodian and repaired or replaced on a schedule. Fox example, the custodian can replace all classroom and hallway lighting dead bulbs on Mondays. In this way, the custodian can take all the necessary equipment, ladders, and bulbs and take care of the entire school at one time instead of dragging out all this equipment several times a week.

PERIODIC CLEANING/MAINTENANCE

The last example suggests that there are some tasks which can be scheduled on a periodic basis instead of doing them every day or as needed. These items include:

- washing windows and cleaning windows within doors
- cleaning areas which become soiled after a period of time—portions of walls where students touch, for example
- cleaning furniture in the faculty lounge
- polishing hallways, cafeteria, and other areas
- finishing gymnasium floor
- cleaning swimming pool bottom
- mowing school lawn, trimming bushes, inspecting athletic fields
- inspection of heating/cooling and other equipment; cleaning of return air grills, univents, and warm air grills

Some tasks are not done daily, but must be done on a regularly scheduled basis. Some of these will be scheduled weekly: mowing and cleaning windows, for example, while others like finishing the gymnasium may only be done once or twice a year. The principal should make a list of what needs to be done and divide the list into those things which should be scheduled on a frequent basis, like once a week, and those which are scheduled less frequently. Then, the principal needs to do two things: (1) for each task, state how often it is to be done; and (2) schedule time into the custodian's day to accomplish these tasks. (Note, again, the 8:00 AM assignment for the custodian as shown in Figure 3.1.)

BUILDING VS. CENTRAL (DISTRICT) OFFICE

Different school districts organize their custodian/maintenance staffs in different ways. In some districts, all the custodians are located at the building level and are responsible to the building principal. There are no central office maintenance staff and no district supervisor. Another school district may assign all custodians to the principals but have one or two maintenance people at the central level reporting to a director of building and grounds (or similar title). Still another district, a larger one, may have all custodians report to a head custodian and have a large group of maintenance people—carpenters, engineers, maintenance personnel – reporting to a central office administrator. Some districts may have both *custodians* and *janitors* with different job descriptions.

In the first case, there is no conflict between school and central office because there are no central office people involved in maintenance. In the second case, there may be conflicts because both the principal and director of buildings and grounds may give instructions to custodians and maintenance personnel. With a head custodian, the conflict may come from the opinion of the principal that he/she has no involvement in the cleanliness and maintenance of the building, and yet seems to feel responsible for everything that occurs in the building.

Thus, in many districts, there can be a conflict between the building principal and the central office person in charge of maintenance. Here are a couple of examples.

(1) Principal John Smith wants to have Mary, his custodian, clean up some spills in the cafeteria but finds that the central office director has told Mary to be at the school's loading dock to receive some supplies. The spill needs to be cleaned now, but Mary is busy somewhere else.

(2) Principal Joan Blair wants her custodian, John, to wax the hallways before an open house, but finds that John has been assigned by the central office to accompany all the other district custodians in accomplishing some district project away from the building.

It is true that both problems could have been solved by appropriate communication and cooperation. But, the point is that this did not occur, and it is quite typical in many districts. Often, it falls to the superintendent or an assistant to bring principals and the central office administrator together to discuss problems, and to develop some procedure and timetable so that both principal and district administrator can be sure their goals can be accomplished.

One step in accomplishing this, if there is a central maintenance staff, is to agree on what is the responsibility of the building custodian and what is the responsibility of the central office maintenance staff. Figure 3.4 contains a partial list of maintenance tasks for each level.

PREVENTIVE MAINTENANCE

The prior section on cleaning and maintenance discussed the necessity for scheduling certain activities such as window washing and gymnasium

Repair leaky drinking fountains and faucets.
Work on minor plumbing problems.
Replace light bulbs and make minor electrical repairs.
Replace fuses and breakers.
Inspect heating/cooling equipment for problems.
Remove snow and ice from areas adjacent to building.
Mow areas around buildings and in inner court.
Respond to work orders submitted to the office.
Repair broken windows, doors, and lockers.

Maintenance List for the Central Office Maintenance Staff

Regularly monitor and repair heating/cooling equipment.
Mow all school grounds away from the buildings.
Remove ice and snow from parking lots and school roads.
Maintain athletic fields.
Respond to plumbing and electrical work which cannot be done by the school custodians.
Carry out the district's preventive maintenance program.

Figure 3.4 *Maintenance List (Partial) for the Building Custodian.*

finishing during the year. In addition to these activities, it is also advisable to schedule other maintenance activities which, if done correctly and on a regular basis, should prevent serious (and costly) breakdowns in building equipment such as heating units, cooling equipment, and fans. This process is called preventive maintenance.

Preventive maintenance is usually seen as a process of inspections with the goal of assuring that "components of the facility remain totally operational and functional according to manufacturer specifications" (Kowalski, 1989, p. 157). Through such an ongoing program, schools can avoid the breakdown of their mechanical systems and any serious deterioration of the building (Castaldi, 1982). Preventive maintenance programs often require extensive data on the facility, as well as people qualified to interpret the data and to perform the appropriate servicing. As a result, many schools have avoided preventive maintenance programs (Morris, 1981) even though computers can be used to compile the data base, sometimes using inventory files (Borowski, 1984; Stronge, 1987).

Most preventive maintenance plans are developed through the cooperation of the district's central office with the architect, a heating and plumbing engineer, an electrical engineer, and a structural engineer. This team can examine the building and give the district a computer printout of what needs to be done and when it should be done. The district can do the work itself if it has the expertise, or it can hire a firm to come in and do the maintenance work. Many schools have chosen not to participate in a preventive maintenance program because of its short-term costs in labor, parts, and, possibly, training. These schools hope that all the equipment holds together for another school year, and that any breakdowns occur during vacations, preferably in the summer. If a district does decide to invest in the future by using preventive maintenance, it is usually the responsibility of the building principal to see that the head custodian performs all the work called for in the preventive maintenance plan (Castaldi, 1982). An example of part of a preventive maintenance schedule is shown in Figure 3.5. Note that this list only shows what should be inspected and when. It does not contain information on the actual maintenance to be performed, or the parts to be replaced. That listing would be more detailed than the list presented. Such a list can be computer-generated and contain cost and time estimates as well as a schedule for replacement and maintenance.

Equipment	Jan	Feb	Mar	Apr	May	June	Jul	Aug	Sept
Boiler—clean								X	
Boiler—inspect	X	X	X	X					
Hot water pumps	X	X	X	X					
Univents									X
Thermostats									X
Pneumatic controls	X	X	X	X	X	X	X	X	X
Roof exhaust		X			X			X	
Roof inspection				X					X
Elect. panel boxes		X			X			X	
Air conditioning controls					X	X	X	X	X
Kitchen exhaust	X		X		X				
Bleacher inspect.									
gym	X	X						X	X
stadium				X					X

***Figure 3.5** A Preventive Maintenance Schedule (Partial).*

THE BUILDING WALK-THROUGH

While these preventive maintenance plans are certainly important to the efficient running of the school machinery, this section suggests expanding the concept of preventive maintenance to one which will help protect the health and safety of the people in the building, especially the students. At the same time, this plan can help reduce the chance of lawsuits against the school district.

One reason schools get sued is because they are charged with negligence. A court looks at a case and judges whether the school staff member or the school board took action that the average, reasonably prudent person would take in the same circumstances. Failure to exercise this care is considered negligence.

At one time, government institutions like schools were immune from tort liability under the concept that "The king can do no wrong." This is no longer true (Alexander and Alexander, 1985).

Let us look at an actual example of a school maintenance problem which could have been prevented but which led, instead, to a successful lawsuit against the school.

In a 1978 incident (*Wilkinson* v. *Hartford*), a twelve-year-old boy (David Wilkinson) was participating in a physical education class in the school gymnasium. He and other students went to the lobby of the gym to get a drink of water during class. While there, David and another boy raced from one end of the lobby to the other end to determine the order they should be positioned when they returned to the gym for the next relay race. David reached the end of the lobby, pushed against a glass panel, and fell outside through the broken glass.

While the court found the teacher was not negligent, it did find the school board negligent. The reason? The school had replaced a similar panel at the other end of the lobby with safety glass after a person had walked through the plate glass panel. The school board was found liable because it had actual knowledge of a condition unreasonably hazardous to its students and did not remedy the situation. In other words, the board did not take the action that an average, reasonably prudent person would have taken in the same circumstances.

Decisions like this mean that school administrators must inspect the condition of the buildings and grounds, identify areas which need to be repaired or changed, and follow through to make certain that the work is completed. This is the expanded concept of preventive maintenance as presented here—to inspect the buildings and grounds on a regular basis (just like the mechanical systems are inspected) and repair and document those areas which are found to be hazardous.

Again, it is the building principal who needs to assume the responsibility for this preventive maintenance, and oversee the work of the custodians in inspecting and correcting the deficiencies.

For a preventive maintenance plan to work, there must be cooperation and a sense of ownership from all involved. Principals and custodians who are new to the building should be given a background sketch of the age of the building, the size and boundaries of the school grounds, the number of rooms and their uses, and the size and capacities of facilities such as the gymnasium, cafeteria, and auditorium. It is also wise to inform these people about the latest dollar valuation of the school property. This orientation should give these new people a sense of ownership in the buildings as they begin their jobs.

An integral part of this expanded concept of preventive maintenance is the building and grounds walk-through. Once a week, the building principal and head custodian should walk the school and the grounds to find potential problems. If it is a large facility, then the building walk-through can be done in wings on a rotating basis throughout the year. The important thing is to establish a list of places to inspect and do it on a regular basis.

The purpose of the walk-through is to inspect the facility, identify areas which need repairs or which are hazardous to health or safety, and see that previously identified hazards have been eliminated since the last inspection. Just as the usual concept of preventive maintenance prevents breakdowns of the school's equipment, this expanded concept of preventive maintenance prevents injury involving (and lawsuits from) the school's inhabitants. In addition to this main purpose, the building walk-through also shows the teachers that someone cares about their working environment and demonstrates to the custodians that someone is checking on their regular cleaning work and on their preventive maintenance repair work.

A typical walk-through is usually done with a notebook to write down areas where potential needs are felt. Some administrators prefer to use small tape recorders, but the comments noted in writing can provide a paper trail which may be useful. Rather than start with a blank notebook, it is better to have a checklist of items to be examined each time. The principal can modify this list and add to it as necessary. After each walk-through, this list should be filed for checking the next time. The checklist might include such items as:

- for hallways – condition of floors, lockers, ceiling tiles; locks and panic bars; lights; dust, dirt, and water on the floors; glass panels; stairways
- for classrooms – chalkboards and tackboards; lights, electrical equipment and plugs; furniture (broken parts, loose sections); ventilation; curtains and blinds; windows; sinks and drains
- special areas – the art room, the industrial arts room, physical education rooms, science labs, home economics, the school kitchen, and restrooms

Each special area has unique purposes, special equipment, and, if not in proper working order, dangerous equipment. These areas need to be included on the checklist and checked carefully.

In addition to rooms frequented by students, the checklist needs to include such areas as incinerator rooms and boiler rooms. Check to see that equipment is working properly and that no one is storing such objects as papers, oily rags, gasoline cans and aerosol cans in these areas.

Many administrators and custodians forget dangers that may exist outside the building. The walk-through should not stop at the building doors but extend into the school grounds as well. Check the trees to see if there are low, overhanging branches that can hurt someone walking or playing nearby. Also, the walkways need to be checked for significant cracks, broken concrete, and other hazards. Open drains can be a problem as can ditches, gratings, and holes which have mysteriously appeared in the schoolyard, In addition, when walking around, look for loose stones or pieces of bricks around shrubbery, flower beds, or windows. These loose objects can result in injury from tripping or from being thrown. Another potential problem are electrical outlets used for outside trimming. Each should have a cover on it, preferably of the locking variety, and should be fitted with a ground fault interrupter.

When outside, check outdoor lighting, school signs, parking areas, fences, playing fields, and (for elementary schools) playground equipment. Many of today's lawsuits result from injuries to students using school playground equipment and playing fields. Be sure to include these areas on the walk-through checklist.

Maintaining a safe and healthy school environment is no longer just a moral and ethical concern, but also a legal concern for today's educators.

Date of inspection______________________________

People involved in inspection____

Area Inspected	Comments	Follow-Up Check
Classrooms		
Chalkboards		
Bulletin boards		
Ceilings		
Lights		
Electrical		
Student desks		
Teacher desks/tables		
Ventilation systems		
Windows		
Curtains/blinds		
Hallways		
Floors		
Students lockers		
Drinking fountains		
Ceiling tiles		
Lights		
Stairways		
Art room		
Kiln		
Tabletops		
Sinks		
Storage		
Kitchen		
Sinks		
Drains		
Freezers		
Lights		
Floor		
Ventilation		
Disposals		
Restrooms		
Floor		
Toilets		
Sinks		
Mirrors		
Dispensers		
Drains		
Stalls/doors		

Figure 3.6 *Building Walk-Through.*

Date of inspection______________________		
People involved in inspection______________________		
Area Inspected	Comments	Follow-Up Check
Outside areas		
Shrubbery/trees		
Signs		
Lighting		
Sidewalks/curbs		
Parking/sidewalks		
Fencing		
Bricks/stones/rocks		
Elect. outlets		
Playground equipment		
Athletic fields		
Outside faucets		

Figure 3.6 (continued).

Since the Illinois Supreme Court (*Molitor* v. *Kaneland*, 1959) ended school district immunity from tort liability, school administrators have increasingly become targets of litigation. Though the risk of lawsuits cannot be eliminated, this expanded concept of preventive maintenance can reduce the frequency and severity of school accidents. With a little preventive maintenance, administrators can eliminate potential hazards, reduce lawsuits, and establish safe, healthy school environments. The key to all of this is planning—preventive maintenance—that allows the administration to stay on top of what is happening within each building. The steps administrators take today can save time, embarrassment, money, trouble, and possibly even lives in the future. An example of a building walk-through list is shown in Figure 3.6.

EMERGENCY PLANS FOR A BUILDING

Building principals should have emergency files in their desks, with plans for possible emergencies. This file might have sections concerning fires, storms, earthquakes (or tornados or hurricanes, depending on area), school strikes, and facilities. The purpose of the file is to provide immediate information to the principal. While the information could be put on the principal's computer, there should also be a hard copy in the desk, since this information may be needed when there is no electricity.

Some of the information contained in the file might include:

(1) Fire—phone numbers of fire department and police; list of people to notify immediately (superintendent, other central office personnel, etc.); list of bus drivers and phone numbers (unless central office calls them to pick up children early); the school evacuation plan; the fire drill plan; and things to take from building during a fire. This last item needs some explanation: Obviously, the most important thing is for people to get out safely. With that priority in mind, someone should be trained to automatically take things like computer disks containing student grades and attendance. All such school records should be kept in duplicate in a vault or other safe place, to be grabbed and taken out of the building by the assigned person. Thought should have been given, before the fire, to where school can be held if the building is burned or damaged in a storm. A few hours of study can result in a document with ideas for the temporary school being placed in this file.

(2) Storms, earthquakes—many of the same items listed above could be repeated here. There are some additional concerns. The building may be fine but have no electricity. In fact, this happens often. The file should have the procedures for dealing with a dark building—move students to new areas? Restrict access to some areas? Cancel lunch? Limit or eliminate after-school events? Are the restrooms too dark? Is the building too cold? Again, discussion at administrator or teacher meetings can clarify these procedures. They should be put into writing and filed for future reference. Schools located in areas which may have special problems (tornados, hurricanes, earthquakes) need to give attention to the preparations which can help in the event of an incident. There are professionally prepared materials designed to help people prepare for each of these possibilities. The principal should obtain this information and select that which is appropriate for the emergency file. For example, information on earthquakes lists items which you should have available in a classroom or in the building, and ways to prepare for an earthquake.

(3) School strikes—Organizations like school board associations, superintendent groups, and principal organizations have printed information on preparing for school strikes and procedures to follow during a strike. While the overall strike procedures have to come from the board of education and the superintendent, the principal

can keep this information in the emergency file, and can be alert to things which he/she might have to address, such as: extracurricular activities, including athletics and athletic practices, evening schools held in the building, special education/vocational education classes held outside the building, security of the building, receiving of commodities and supplies during a strike, transportation of staff and students, laws on picketing, district policy on dealing with the press, and food service in the building. Even if the principal does not have the final say on many of these items, it is still beneficial to have studied this material, and to be able to contribute to discussions at the administrative meetings on a pending school strike.

(4) Bomb threats—The administration should discuss this potential problem and develop a district policy and procedures for dealing with such a threat. Communications are important—Who is notified? What information is shared? What are the teachers and staff told? Who contacts the police? If searching for the bomb is part of the procedures, who performs the search? How open is the search? Who can train the people who will do the searching if they are staff members? Also, some schools have coded messages that can be relayed to teachers, either in person or over the intercom, to alert them to the threat. Most school districts will have a bomb threat at some time, though not usually an actual bomb. Thus, each principal needs to have a set of procedures available in the emergency file.

(5) Facilities—Finally, there should be some items regarding facilities in the emergency file. Here are some items suggested by Lane and Betz (1987) as things a principal should know. They are very appropriate for the file.

- location of controls for heating, cooling, water, lighting, clocks
- location of circuit breakers and all alarm systems
- location of blueprints for the building
- fire and disaster drill formats
- location of master keys and spare keys for the building
- information on the operation of the telephone system and the public address system
- information on who to contact (with telephone numbers) for the above items

If the district has a telephone directory of all staff, place a copy of that in the file. Also, if some administrators have unlisted office or home numbers, have those available. (Unlisted office numbers? Yes, sometimes it is helpful to have, in addition to the public numbers, unlisted and unpublished private office phone numbers for each principal and the superintendent. These people can then communicate with each other directly on lines unknown to anyone else and almost always available.)

ESTIMATING NUMBER OF CLASSROOMS NEEDED

Estimating the number of classrooms needed at the elementary school using a self-contained model is fairly simple—divide the number of second graders, for example, by the appropriate class size (where appropriate class size can mean the principal's opinion, tradition, negotiated class size, etc.). Or, working backward, principals may simply divide the students by the number of classrooms (or teachers). The number of classrooms needed will always work out with this latter method!

It is more complicated at high schools (and some junior highs) where students sign up for individual courses. How can a principal determine the number of classrooms needed for all English classes, for example, in a high school of 500 students? Nelson (1972) developed a formula to estimate the classrooms needed (some of the symbols have been changed):

$$CR = (E \times PW)/(A \times MS \times SO)$$

where

CR = number of *classrooms* needed
E = anticipated *enrollment*
PW = number of *periods* a class meets per *week*
A = number of different *activities* in the same space at the same time (a gym could have more than one class at a time)
MS = *maximum* class *size* allowed
SO = percentage of time (as a decimal) that you want the *space occupied*

Example

For this example, we have 500 high school students (E), each meeting in class for five periods a week (PW). Since this is for English classes (not physical education, for example), only one activity (English class) will occur in each classroom (*A*). The maximum class size (*MS*) for English has been determined to be twenty-five for this example. To determine the time that the room should be occupied or scheduled (*SO*), multiply the maximum possible class periods by the desired percentage: At this school, there are six periods a day for classes for five days a week, or thirty class periods. Although using rooms for 100 percent of the time would seem to be the most efficient, principals do need rooms for other uses during the school day. In this example, the principal decided to occupy rooms 90 percent of the time in order to have some flexibility. 90 percent of 30 class periods = 27

$$CR = (E \times PW)/(A \times MS \times SO)$$
$$CR = (500 \times 5)/(1 \times 25 \times 27)$$
$$CR = (2{,}500)/675)$$
$$CR = 3.7$$

The principal should allow for four classrooms for the English classes in the high school.

USE OF COMPUTERS FOR FACILITY MANAGEMENT

Mention has already been made for several uses of the computer. The determination of the number of classrooms needed, as just presented, certainly can be done easily on a computer. Earlier, it was suggested that the preventive maintenance program could be scheduled by a computer, including what to do, when to do it, what equipment or supplies are needed, how much it will cost, and how long it should take to complete the procedure. Using a data base, the principal can put part of the emergency file on the computer (making sure to keep a hard copy in the desk) and can keep track of items to be repaired as a result of the regular building walk-through. Still another use of the computer is to use a data base to keep track of the building inventory of equipment. Initially, the principal will have to take an inventory of every major item in the building and log the name of the item and its location in the data base. Some schools go a step further in marking each item with a number which is also entered into the computer. As new equipment is purchased, this information can be placed into the computer with any additional desired information, such as the cost of the item and the purchase date. Using the data base, the principal can call up the information in any

Item Purchased	Date Purchased	Cost of Item	Assigned Location of Item
Desk	7/31/88	254.00	Perry High 102
Desk	5/6/78	140	Perry High 103
Desk	3/6/88	234.00	Central Office 24
Chair	8/7/90	345	Central Office 24
Chair	7/8/89	217	Johnson Elem. 105
Chair	6/5/87	278	Johnson Elem. 101
Computer #417	8/6/90	485	Johnson Elem. 102
Computer #400	7/6/86	875	Central Office 24
Computer #375	9/7/90	1,250	Johnson Elem. 103

Here are the same items listed according to item (computers).

Item Purchased	Date Purchased	Cost of Item	Assigned Location of Item
Computer #375	9/7/90	1,250	Johnson Elem. 103
Computer #400	7/6/86	875	Central Office 24
Computer #417	8/6/90	485	Johnson Elem. 102

Here are the same items listed according to location (Central Office 24).

Item Purchased	Date Purchased	Cost of Item	Assigned Location of Item
Desk	3/6/88	234.00	Central Office 24
Chair	8/7/90	345	Central Office 24
Computer #400	7/6/86	875	Central Office 24

All of these lists came from the same data base. The computer can be asked to sort these items according to any desired category.

Figure 3.7 Examples of Data Base Inventory Printouts.

order–by the equipment name (all typewriters, for example, regardless of location), the location (all equipment located in the office or in room 201), or by the purchase date, etc. An example of this type of information is given in Figure 3.7.

AN ALTERNATIVE—CONTRACTING OUT SERVICES

One alternative to having the district's own employees provide a service is to contract out the service to a private company. Many school districts contract maintenance, food service, and/or pupil transportation. Each district needs to examine its own ability to supply the service and look at the advantages and disadvantages for that district. Here are some of the advantages which some districts find in contracting out services:

(1) There are no unions or negotiating. Since the people providing the

service are not school employees, the school district does not have to deal with negotiations, grievances, or employee unions. Often, the employees of the private firms are not unionized, and even if they are, the unions are affiliated with the private company, not the school district.

(2) The responsibility is clear. Often in smaller districts, no one has overall responsibility for providing the service. For example, the small district may not have a director of buildings and grounds or head of maintenance. While the superintendent has the responsibility, he/she is also responsible for everything else, and maintenance may not be high on the superintendent's agenda or high on his/her list of expertise. When services are contracted out, the company puts a person in charge of the service, someone who has the responsibility for the service—and who is not responsible for anything else.

(3) The school may lack expertise. While the district may have custodians who can clean satisfactorily, it may not have anyone who can handle preventive maintenance, or plan and organize the custodians into teams to execute any periodic maintenance functions. Similarly, the district, lacking the expertise, may not have the correct or up-to-date equipment for many jobs. The company contracted for building maintenance will provide someone with expertise to train the staff, supervise the work to be done, and provide the necessary equipment at the company's expense. (The equipment remains the property of the company, of course.)

(4) It can save money. Most companies who provide services can show that they can provide the service at a lower price. Lieberman (1986) states that in private companies, thrift, economy, and the bottom line are more important than they are in schools. He feels that these private companies will find ways to provide the service at a savings to the school. Moreover, he feels that these cost-saving methods and attitudes of business will spill over into the school district in other activities.

Since most school districts still provide services through their own employees, there must be some advantages to this, and some disadvantages to contracting out services. Here are some of the disadvantages:

(1) The company employees are not district employees. There is often

a very beneficial relationship between the principal and the custodian, the cook and the teacher, the bus driver and the assistant principal. When the workers providing these services are not school district employees, this relationship may be lost to some extent. The loyalty of a worker is usually to the people who hire, pay and evaluate the employee. That person works for a private company, not the school district, when services are contracted out. Earlier in the chapter there was discussion of the conflict that can arise between the school principal and the central office maintenance person (when one exists). In that discussion, both administrators were school district employees reporting to the same superintendent. When services are contracted out, the central office maintenance person is not a school employee. The conflict discussed can become worse, and the solution (meeting with the superintendent) is not as easy, since one person does not report to the superintendent as a district employee.

(2) Expenditures may be harder to control. While the overall costs may be lower, as stated earlier, individual expenditures may be harder to control. For example, when services are provided by district employees, there is a budget for expenditures for the service which is provided. A district employee requests supplies, equipment or repairs, and the administrator decides whether to approve them. When the services are contracted out, the requests for supplies and repairs (equipment is usually provided by the company) come from someone who is not a district employee. This supervisor is not concerned with the district's budget, but with the ability to perform the service. In general, the more supplies and repairs that can be purchased or done, the better the job that can be done. Also, the outside supervisor has a contractual edge. He/she can state that in order to have the staff perform up to the specifications or guarantees of the contract with the district, certain expenditures are necessary. To refuse these expenditures may invalidate the contract, the outside supervisor may claim.

(3) There are political problems. While most district-employed maintenance personnel, cooks, and bus drivers are local residents, a private company can use its own staff, although it usually retains the district's staff initially. There is a fear locally that all the staff will be shipped in from afar, and no local people will be hired. Also, if the private company is unionized and the staff goes on strike, the

school district administration is not in a position to solve the problem as it is with district employees.

A Case Study

One of the authors, while a superintendent in Indiana, used contracted services. This is a brief description of that experience.

One of the board members, in charge of facilities at a large Indianapolis hospital, suggested that the district investigate the possibility of contracting out services for maintenance and food services. Although the board of education decided to keep the current arrangement for food services, it did decide to contract out maintenance.

The first step was to locate and invite representatives from several companies to make presentations to the board of education. Following these presentations, the board members and the superintendent visited the companies at their headquarters and later talked to people who used their services. The companies examined the district budget and staffing, and made proposals, explaining exactly what services they would provide, with what staff, and at what cost to the district. The costs were below the amount spent by the district for personnel wages and benefits, supplies, and equipment. The board picked one of the companies and signed a contract for maintenance services. The company was paid monthly, and the contract specified the fixed monthly cost. On the night the board of education approved the contract, it also released all of the custodial/maintenance staff as district employees. The company which the board had selected agreed to hire all of these employees at their current salaries the next day. The following morning, the superintendent and company representative met with all of the affected employees to explain the changes and assure them that they were still employed, although not by the district. The company brought in a full-time supervisor to train the staff, work with the superintendent, and represent the company. At first, there were some problems, as the employees did not like the board's decision and were, understandably, anxious about the new arrangement and supervisor. One of the unanticipated problems was the issue of accumulated sick leave and vacation leave. When the staff asked the new company what would happen to these accumulated benefits, they were told that they had no accumulated benefits because they were new employees. The board of education eventually paid these benefits in cash to the employees since they could not take leave (earned with the school district) with the new employer. The decision to switch to contracted services for maintenance was made in 1983 and, according to supporters and former critics alike, it has been a success and is still in existence as of this book's publication.

SUMMARY

This chapter discussed the role of the building principal in maintaining the school facility. Cleaning, maintenance, avoidance of hazards in the building and on the grounds, emergency plans, and preventive maintenance were among the topics included in the chapter. The following chapter will discuss public relations, both inside the building with the staff and students, and outside the building with the parents and community.

THE PRINCIPAL'S CASEBOOK

The Case of the Wiggling Wire

In making your usual weekly building walk-through, you found a loose electrical wire in an outside receptacle. Because you are not much of an electrician, you are not sure how dangerous it is or whether it is even live. You know enough not to touch it, however. Some kids in your elementary school are playing outside and a rubber ball bounces off the building a few feet from this receptacle. Your custodian is probably cleaning up in the cafeteria or eating somewhere himself.

Questions to Consider

- What do you do first? Next? After that?
- Should this have been caught earlier?
- Who is responsible for seeing it?
- Can you leave the area?
- Should you?

REFERENCES

Alexander, K. and M. D. Alexander. 1985. *American Public School Law.* St. Paul: West Publishing Co.

Borowski, P. 1984. "Maintaining A Computerized Building File," *CEPF Journal*, 22(5):18.

Castaldi, B. 1982. *Educational Facilities*. Boston: Allyn and Bacon.

Kowalski, T. J. 1989. *Planning and Managing School Facilities*. New York: Praeger Publishers.

Lane, K. and L. Betz. 1987. "The Principal New to a School–What Questions to Ask about the Facility," *NASSP Bulletin*, 71(502):125–127.

Lieberman, M. 1986. *Beyond Public Education*. New York: Praeger.

Molitor v. *Kaneland Community Unit District No. 302*, 1959. 18 ILL2d 11, 163 N.E. 2d 89.

Morris, J. 1981. "Developing A Small Scale Preventive Maintenance Program," *American School and University*, 53(8):15.

Nelson, N. 1972. "Performance Specifications: Determining Space Requirements," Unpublished Paper, Purdue University, West Lafayette, Indiana.

Sharp, W. L. and J. K. Walter. 1992. "Preventative Maintenance: Toward An Expanded Concept," *The Educational Facility Planner*, 30(4):11–13.

Stronge, J. 1987. "The School Building Principal and Inventory Control," *CEPF Journal*, 25(6):4–6.

Wilkinson v. *Hartford Accident and Indemnity Co.*, 1982. 411 So. 2d 22.

CHAPTER 4

Public Relations

INTRODUCTION

To many people, *public relations* means promoting the school throughout the community and fostering and nourishing a positive relationship between the school and the citizens of the community. While this is an important part of public relations (and will be included in this chapter), it only constitutes half the public relations program. The first half should start in the school itself—internal relations among the various individuals and groups represented in the school and in the school district.

The superintendent of schools, under the direction of policies set by the board of education, must take a lead in the pursuit of good public relations, both inside and outside the district. This book, however, is concentrating on the principal's various roles, and therefore will not discuss the role of the superintendent or school board, except to state that the principal needs to be aware of these roles, and be aware of what role the superintendent wants the building principals to play in public relations.

First, to have good external public relations, the school needs to have good internal relations. The teachers, custodians, secretaries, and other staff members represent the school to many people outside the building. How these people feel about their jobs, the progress of the school, the behavior of the children, and the curriculum of the school is communicated directly or indirectly to parents and other local citizens.

INTERNAL RELATIONS

What would promote internal morale? What would make employees more satisfied with their overall situation? A couple of studies might suggest some answers. George Mason University (1982) studied employer-employee desires, and found that while the employer thought the most important desires of the employees were good pay, job security, and promotion, the employees themselves listed their goals as interesting work, an appreciation of their work, and a feeling of being in on things. Another report stated that employee needs included five major areas—the opportunity to do something significant, recognition that they made the most of this opportunity, a sense of belonging and being a part of things, economic security, and emotional security (Executive Reports Corporation, 1971).

SUGGESTIONS FOR THE PRINCIPAL

The principal must be in charge of the internal relations program in the building. The program should include carefully planned aspects as well as very informal aspects. The goal should be tied to the research stated earlier—to make people feel that what they do is important, to recognize people for their work, and to make them feel a part of the process and progress of the school. Following are some suggestions for the principal to consider when developing the internal relations program.

Treat People Fairly

Everyone wants to feel that they are treated fairly. Sometimes, if the principal would only explain why he/she took some action, the action would be perceived as fair. It is so easy to issue an edict, send a memorandum, or tell someone to deliver a message to someone else. Often, the receiver of these instructions gets upset simply because no one explained the motivation behind the instructions—no one took the time to talk to him or her personally. It does take extra time to talk to individuals, explain what is going on, and ask for their help. Think of the difference between:

- Principal Smith realizes that he needs a teacher to supervise an area on short notice and drops a note into John's mailbox telling him to report to that location at 2:00 PM to supervise.
- Principal Jones realizes that she needs a teacher to supervise an area on short notice and speaks directly to Mary, telling her that

there is a special need, that she knows Mary has a busy schedule, and she really needs her help today.

While both John and Mary are inconvenienced by the assignment and neither may like having it, Mary at least understands the situation and has been told by the principal that she is needed. People want to be treated fairly, and part of that fair treatment is explaining things to them. Most staff members, if they think they have not been treated fairly, think they have been treated quite differently than someone else in the same circumstances. Taking the time to talk and explain situations minimizes this feeling.

Clarify Roles

An earlier chapter discussed what can happen when a principal and a central office administrator assign a custodian to do two different tasks at the same time. It causes confusion and conflicting loyalties, and it results in power plays. Everyone needs to know what his or her role is: what is supposed to be done, when it's to be done, and who is responsible for giving instructions. For many in the building, it is obviously the principal who is the immediate boss. However, for some it can be confusing—for the custodian just discussed, for the teacher who works in more than one building, or for the special education or remedial teacher who also reports to another person. These and other staff members need to feel secure in their jobs and in their professional relationships. The principal needs to make sure he/sure understands the relationships, and then needs to discuss them with the people who are in this situation.

Open Up Communications, Part 1

Obviously this is related to the above points, but is also something more. A principal may say there is an open door policy in the office, but the frown on the principal's face, or the stern look of the secretary, may bring that open door policy into question. Staff members know whether the principal really wants them to come in and talk about concerns or questions. The attitude of the principal becomes apparent and everyone knows what it is. If the principal smiles, welcomes staff members, even gets up to greet them sometimes, or comes out of the office to say hello to someone in the outer office, staff members will notice it and remember it. And, mentioning the secretary is not just an accident. If the secretary takes her gatekeeping responsibilities too seriously, she may prevent a well-meaning principal from having the open door policy which the principal described to the staff. On a personal note, one of the authors of this book had one of his secretaries tell a bus driver, "Dr. Sharp does not want to see you." It happened that Dr. Sharp did not even know the bus driver was there, and certainly had never given those instructions to the secretary. The driver was a relative of a school board member and Dr. Sharp was the superintendent. When the school board member heard this, he did not believe it sounded like the superintendent's usual behavior, so he talked with him and they both discovered that the secretary had taken on this responsibility without any instructions. This incident started an investigation and resulted in the dismissal of the secretary. Had the bus driver not been related to the board member, he could simply have spread the word with many other staff members that the superintendent did not want to talk to them, at least not to bus drivers.

Open Up Communications, Part 2

Get out of the office. Principals have so much work to do, so many phone calls, so much paper work, and so many students and staff members who come to the office that they could sit behind that big desk all day long and keep very busy. But the principal cannot do that. Principals need to get out of the office and into the places where other people work—classrooms, cafeterias, gyms, lounges, hallways, and outside the building. These times should not just be when principals have to be there to evaluate someone or to deliver a message. They need to be there without an agenda, to be accessible, to talk to people, to observe the school in action, to pat someone on the back, or to wave to someone in the distance. The principal is the leader, and a leader should be seen. It is fine to formalize some contacts, like going to student council meetings or sending questionnaires to seniors or graduates to seek their opinions about the school. There are very good reasons to do these things. The principal needs the informal contacts, too, since many school people will not be in the student council or respond to a formal questionnaire. The principal can also meet with the faculty without having a formal faculty meeting. An effective technique is to invite faculty members to meet after school, without the usual agenda, and ask for their comments about the school. Stick to the plan and do not make announcements, hand out materials, or give speeches. Invite them to come, and let them talk about their concerns. Note that this section mentioned students. Sometimes the principal, in thinking about internal relations, thinks only about the teachers or only about the staff members. Students must be included in these thoughts about internal relations as well.

Open Up Communications, Part 3

Yes, communication is so important it takes three parts to discuss. "If principals want to be sure a message they have sent has been received and interpreted in the intended way, they should question and receive feedback to determine the accuracy of perception" (Wood, Nicholson, and Findley, 1985, p. 108). Certainly, principals need to send out bulletins, make announcements over the intercom system (but so often?), and support an internal newsletter for the staff. But, as this quote says, it is important to have follow-up to see if the message sent was the one received. If the important word for real estate people is location, location, location, the word for principals is communication, communication, communication.

Recognize Groups and Individuals

There are many ways to do both informally with a pat on the back and formally with a recognition program. The principal needs to know the school staff well before establishing a formal recognition program. What is successful and well-received at one school may be considered an insult in another. One of the authors, a superintendent of a district with four high schools, asked each principal to come up with some way to recognize outstanding teachers. Two principals chose to do the same thing—have the faculty select an outstanding teacher for the year and recognize that teacher publicly with pictures and a story. One school faculty liked the idea and followed through, selecting a very good teacher to honor. The other school faculty refused to participate, stating that they were all outstanding and could not select one teacher as any better than the others.

Here are some ideas which have been used successfully in particular schools: a birthday card sent to the home of each staff member with a short personal message from the administrator; a party with a cake for all the cooks (not baked by the cooks) or all the bus drivers or the teacher aides, with a short thank you from the principal; a pen or plaque given to staff members who have been with the school for five years, ten years, etc., and a reserved parking place with a special sign for a month for someone who has been selected for an achievement. There are many other similar ideas which principals use. The main thing is to decide what is appropriate and what would really be appreciated. For example, making staff members come to an 8 PM board meeting, dressed up, to shake hands with board members and receive a pen may not be the high point of the week for some staff. On the other hand, the custodian who has been in the school for twenty years may long remember an honor like this. Who is to know what to do? The principal. Talk to people, get their reactions, find out what they appreciate, and be flexible.

Share Decision Making

Share decision making with the staff, to extent that it can be done in your school. The latter qualification is mentioned for several good reasons. Some principals are very open to some types of shared decision making, but would not consider other forms. Some principals have a hard time sharing any decision making with assistants, let along with other staff members. The same range of attitudes is shared by superintendents and board members. If a principal wants to have some form of shared decision making, it is best to check with the superintendent to see what his/her attitude is regarding this form of administration. We should not forget the teachers, who, as individuals, will also have divergent views about the subject. It is not true that all teachers want to be involved in making decisions about the school. Some want to be involved in all decisions, others are happy that selected staff members can be involved (but not them), and still others want to be left alone to teach, letting the principal make the decisions and take the responsibility. Know your superintendent, know your faculty, and know yourself before jumping into any shared decision-making efforts.

SHARED DECISION MAKING, PARTICIPATIVE MANAGEMENT, EMPOWERMENT

Keith and Girling (1991), in discussing participative management, suggest that information should flow both up and down the organization, that ideas need to be shared, and that teachers need to be involved in decision making and in planning for the school. Kanter (cited in the Keith and Girling book, p. 38) feels that empowerment has benefits for both the individual and for the organization, improving productivity for the organization and creating feelings of fulfillment, team identity, and cooperation (with the administration) for the employee. Furthermore, research seems to indicate that there is a significant correlation between participative management and employee satisfaction and organizational productivity. (Miller et al., as mentioned in Keith and Girling, p. 33).

Principals need the support of their staffs to be effective or to make changes in the school. One way to secure support is to have the staff share in decisions so that the goals of the school and the procedures used to reach these goals are not handed down by the administration, but are mutually agreed upon. Harrison (1987) has stated that decisions made by such a cooperative group are better decisions than those made by one person, such as a principal. Not only do principals get better support on decisions through shared decision making, they also get better decisions for the school.

Case Study

There are many ways to involve a staff in making decisions and these are known by different names: shared decision making, participative (or participatory) decision making, teacher empowerment, and others. The extent of the involvement of the staff differs from place to place. Many principals have used a principal's advisory council for years, asking teachers to choose representatives to meet with the principal on a regular basis. What actually happens in these meetings varies from school to school. At one school, the group may be quite involved in discussions, helping the principal make decisions while at another school, the group may spend most of the time listening to the principal explain what he/she intends to do. Needless to say, having an advisory council does not necessarily mean that there is any shared decision making. At the other extreme are examples where teachers are responsible for the decisions and the principal is more of a facilitator.

That is the case at Central-Hower High School in Akron, Ohio, an inner-city school with nearly 1,000 students, 45 percent of whom are black, 45 percent white, and 8 percent of the remainder Asian. In 1984, the faculty, school administration, central administration, and the board of education worked together to formulate a structure to involve the faculty in the decisions of the high school.

While the initial steps were not unique, the faculty became more and more involved in decision making, and this process led to their unique governance system.

Supported by the administration, a Faculty Senate was formed. It consists of the high school principal and eight teachers, elected by members of the eight curricular departments in the school. This Faculty Senate meets every day to consider the decisions which need to be made in the policies of the high school, under a constitution which was approved by the school faculty and the board of education.

Each decision is decided by a vote of the Senate, with each member, including the principal, having one of the nine votes. Because the principal has no veto power over any decision, cannot chair the meeting, and yet has accountability for the school, the constitution allows the principal to appeal a decision to the central administration. Likewise, the high school faculty itself may appeal a decision of the Faculty Senate by petitioning the Senate for a referendum of the faculty. Through the Faculty Senate and the standing committees it has created (finance, evaluation, bylaws, grants, curriculum, professional development), the teachers at Central-Hower have taken a step toward real involvement in decision making beyond the classroom. In research by Childs (1991), it was found that faculty members who were at the school between 1984 and 1990 perceived that they were more involved in decision making in 1990 than in the past, were more willing to take responsibility because their governance structure does not call for token involvement, and perceived that student achievement had increased during that time. (Scores on standardized tests seem to confirm their feelings.) Thus, if teachers are involved in decision making, where their participation is real and where the decisions in which they are involved are significant, then there can be positive results for the teachers and for the students.

EXTERNAL RELATIONS

The principal needs to remember that the superintendent is in charge of the public relations program for the school district. Any program the principal establishes at the school level has to be consistent with that of the district program. Since superintendents and boards of education do not like surprises, the principal should check with the superintendent to be sure that the school's public relations program is acceptable to the central administration.

When establishing a school public relations program, the principal should keep in mind that there are some school events which affect public relations—even if they are not considered a part of the public relations program. For example, public presentations by students, field trips by students and faculty members to community sites, commencement activities, athletic contests, and work-study programs are all examples of activities which most would not associate with a public relations program. However, the school's perception is affected by all aspects of these programs—student behavior, faculty advance arrangements, efficiency of coordination, appearance of the building, etc. Principals should remember that public relations activities occur in many places.

For the formal part of the public relations program, that which is established with certain goals and procedures, the principal might want to consider a faculty committee. Kimbrough and Burkett (1990) suggest using such a committee to develop ideas on public relations for the school, then sharing these ideas with the rest of the faculty. As stated earlier, it is important for the faculty to understand the program and to feel a part of it. In addition, there are many resources available from such organizations as the National School Boards Association and those organizations representing administrator groups.

INFORMATION

One aspect of a school's public relations program is sharing information about the school with the community. This can be done in many ways, and the principal should consider which way is best for different information. Some of these information activities follow.

Open Houses and Parent Conferences

The purpose of open houses and parent conferences is usually to share teachers' views of their students' academic progress with parents. They may also be used to explain the school's programs and activities.

Newsletters from the School

Many schools send newsletters to parents, telling about the recent activities in the school and the events scheduled for the future.

Presentations

On occasion, principals make presentations or ask students to make presentations to the school board and to community groups, and have student groups (like the band or choir) put on programs for community organizations. While part of these presentations may consist of a short performance, part is often an explanation of the program involved (e.g., the music department's offerings).

Parent-Teacher Organizations

Especially at the elementary school level, principals often meet with parent-teacher organizations like the PTA or PTO (Parent-Teacher Association, Parent-Teacher Organization) or similar organization. Recently, the *teacher* part of the title is in name only in many schools, as the meetings tend to be mostly parents and administrators. These meetings give the principal another opportunity to talk about the school and its programs, and to answer questions from the group.

Community Groups

Principals are sometimes asked to address the local Lions Club, Rotary, Kiwanis, etc., to talk about the school. Many school districts have found this important enough to have principals join these groups and take part in the activities instead of just being a guest speaker.

Informal Groups

Some communities establish neighborhood "coffees" so that small groups of people in a certain residential area can get together and meet with the principal to discuss the school.

Senior Citizen Activities

In a more recent development, some schools have invited senior citizens to come into the school for various activities—a lunch, a short musical program, a reading session with certain students, or a grandmother-father's day. In most cases, the activity is supplemented with a visit by the principal who shares information about the school and answers questions.

Parent Lunches

Some principals invite parents of first graders or freshmen (the people in their first year in that building) to have lunch with the principal, or morning coffee with the principal so the principal can speak with a small group of parents each month.

The Media

Certainly, if the topic is information, the media must be mentioned. Principals must know how to work with reporters, know what is a good story to them, know about media timelines, and know what information a reporter needs to have. While there are articles and textbooks written about this topic, this book would suggest that the principal make an appointment with the reporter, possibly over lunch, to discuss these questions. Conditions, such as deadlines and requirements, vary from place to place, and the principal should know what is needed in his/her school's media market. Equally important, it gives the principal and reporter a chance to get to know each other away from the PTA meeting or the board meeting.

INVOLVEMENT WITH COMMUNITY GROUPS

While the sharing of information is crucial to the success of a school's public relations program, it is not sufficient. As Wood, Nicholson, and Findley (1985) state, "Community relations includes involvement as well as information" (p. 111). Not only do principals need to speak to community groups, they need to establish good relationships with the members of those groups. A principal should study the power structure of the community, and know who makes decisions, who people listen to, and who they go to for information.

An alternative to going out to community groups is to invite community members in to meet with the principal. Some principals have advisory committees consisting of parents, community members, leaders, or a combination of these groups. These groups meet periodically and offer an opportunity for the principal to give and receive information and opinions. A related activity, though slightly different, is the key communicator concept. A principal identifies those community members who communicate with many members of the community and invites them to meet with him/her on a regular basis. As Kindred, Bagin, and Gallagher (1990) suggest, this group may have community leaders as usually defined, but may also consist of people such as barbers, beauticians, bartenders, restaurant owners, doctors, and dentists who meet and talk with many people throughout the day.

Two special community groups suggested for involvement with the principal are the business community and, if nearby, the university community. Forming links with the businesses in the community can help in several ways, from field trip sites to resources to expertise. As Keith and Girling (1991) state, "Not only will businesses make in-kind and financial contributions to schools in their community but they can supplement the school's academic program through field-placement opportunities for students who are participating in special academic programs" (p. 260). Similarly, the school can benefit from its relationship and involvement with nearby colleges and universities. Partnerships between the two can help minority student programs, enrichment programs, professional development programs for the teachers and administrators, and the sharing of expertise and experience.

PUBLIC RELATIONS AT THE FRONT DOOR

While all of the above suggestions would contribute to a good public relations program, they could also be relatively useless if the principal ignores how people are treated when they come to visit the school or call the school on the phone. This important aspect of the public relations program is part of an article titled "You Can Improve Your School's Image WITHOUT Spending Money," which is included in this book as Appendix A. Please take a look at it.

COMMUNICATION IS A TWO-WAY STREET

While the beginning of this section on external relations discussed getting information *to* the community, the latter part, detailing the necessity of involving the principal with community groups, raised the concept of getting information *from* the community. It is important for the principal to actively seek information from the parents and the community. One way is through interaction as mentioned earlier.

Another way is to seek information with a questionnaire. "Community surveys provide a wealth of information essential to the success of the public relations effort" (Guthrie and Reed, 1991, p. 364).

The ways in which principals survey members of the community and how they interpret the data received is important. While principals may not want to elicit responses from a true random sample and have their questionnaire checked for validity and reliability, they should still be careful about the overall process. Here are some suggestions:

(1) First, surveys do not have to have written questionnaires. People can be questioned by phone surveys or by interviews as well as by written questionnaire. However, it does take a lot more time and personnel to phone people or to interview them in person. Also, the confidentiality which can be assured in a written questionnaire is lost in the verbal survey, at least to the person making the verbal survey. Once the principal decides upon the format, he/she should check with the superintendent to be sure the survey concept is acceptable. Check again when the questionnaire (or list of verbal survey questions) is ready to be reviewed.

(2) In most cases, principals will send the written questionnaire to all the parents in the school (if parents are being surveyed). However, in a very large school with more limited resources, it might be better to send a random sample. The number of people who need to be surveyed, and the method of picking those people, can be determined by reading some of the references listed for this chapter.

(3) To get the best possible response, the principal should enclose a stamped, self-addressed envelope with the questionnaire instead of having students bring back the questionnaire. In this way, parents know that their responses are confidential. It also shows that the principal is serious about wanting people to respond. Of course, some parents will complain about the school spending the postage, but the principal should be able to defend the charge if the questionnaire asks questions which are important ones, and if the administration acts upon the results.

(4) Be careful about the wording of the questionnaire. Be concise, keep questions and statements simple. Use language that the people being surveyed understand, not "educationese." Pretest the questionnaire by presenting it to the principal's advisory council, or the officers of the PTO, or to another small group which is similar to

the group to which it is being sent. See if this group understands the questions before duplicating all of the copies.

(5) The questionnaire needs a cover letter to explain its purpose. This can also be accomplished by enclosing the questionnaire with the regular newsletter which explains the purpose, or by having a paragraph or two at the top of the questionnaire. In this letter or section, explain who is being surveyed, why, and what use will be made of the results. Thank respondents for taking the time to complete and return the confidential questionnaire.

(6) Do not make it too long or difficult to answer. If you want to be sure very few will respond, make it long and add a lot of questions which are open-ended e.g., "What do you think about the mathematics program?" To be sure that a sufficient number of people respond to make it worthwhile (and meaningful), ask questions which have multiple choice answers or can be answered with one or two words. There is another problem if most of the questions are open-ended—the responses may range all over the place, making it very difficult to draw any conclusions as to the public's position on the issue. It is certainly acceptable to have one or two open-ended questions or a statement such as, "Please make any other comments you wish below." However, these should be placed at the end of the questionnaire. If they are at the beginning, some people will decide not to answer anything and throw away the entire questionnaire. If placed at the end, those same people may mail in the questionnaire with only those questions unanswered.

(7) Be careful about asking any personal or demographic questions. If it is necessary to do so, put them at the end for the same reason as listed above. If the person responding decides not to answer these questions, the questionnaire, already completed, may still be returned. Also, if there is a good reason to ask personal questions such as age or salary (and in most cases it is unnecessary), give the respondents a choice of responses in ranges, such as ages 21–30, 31–40, etc.

(8) Be careful about how the results are interpreted. Keep in mind that the questionnaire probably was not tested for reliability or validity and the number of responses received may not be very large. Thus, the results may give the principal some idea about how some of the parents felt about certain issues, but do not tell the principal that all parents, or even a scientific random sample, feel this way. Again,

be careful not to make more out of the results that can reasonably be made.

(9) Finally, share the results with the public. If they have taken the time to complete the questionnaire, give the results to the newspaper or include them in a school newsletter. Then, make use of the results, if not for specific actions, at least for discussion at faculty meetings or parent advisory committees. Doing this will help get a good response the next time a survey is done. Avoiding these steps will tell people that answering another questionnaire is a waste of time and the school's money.

SUMMARY

This chapter discussed the role of the principal in public relations in the school building and in the community. It also discussed shared decision making in the school, the mechanics of using a questionnaire, and working with community groups outside the school. The next chapter will present the role of the principal in the area of personnel.

THE PRINCIPAL'S CASEBOOK

The Case of the Phony Phone

While away at a conference in the southern part of the country, you called the central office to talk to the superintendent. Instead of a secretary, you received an answer from the newly purchased answering machine. It responded with a few words, obviously in the middle of a sentence, and then said, "You may leave a message in the mailbox." While you recalled that this meant that the school now had voice mail and you could leave a verbal message, you thought about the countless people who called and did not know this. Also, you wondered if the district was closed due to snow since the machine answered the phone. You tried again and got the same result.

Questions to Consider

- Who can you call now?
- Should you tell the superintendent about this communications problem? Now or when you get back?

- Is this a communications problem or is the principal over-reacting?
- How helpful is the recording? Should it only be used when no one is in the building (holiday/snow day) or also when the secretary is taking a break or is at lunch?
- What are the benefits of an answering machine vs. a human voice?

REFERENCES

Childs, S. 1991. "Perceptions of Participative Decision Making, Professionalism, and Job Satisfaction by Central-Hower High School Faculty in Comparison with Other Akron Secondary Teachers," Ed.D. diss., The University of Akron, Ohio.

Executive Reports Corporation. 1971 *Breaking the Communications Barrier.* Englewood Cliffs, N.J.: Prentice-Hall, p. 6.

George Mason University. 1982. "Report of the National School Public Relations Association Staff Renewal Committee," Arlington, VA, p. 8.

Guthrie, J. W. and R. J. Reed. 1991. *Educational Administration and Policy: Effective Leadership for American Education,* Boston: Allyn and Bacon, p. 364.

Harrison, E. F. 1987. *The Managerial Decision-Making Process.* Boston: Houghlin Mifflin Co.

Keith, S. and R. Girling. 1991. *Education, Management, and Participation.* Boston: Allyn and Bacon, pp. 41–42.

Kimbrough, R. B. and C. W. Burkett. 1990. *The Principalship: Concepts and Practices.* Englewood Cliffs, N.J.: Prentice Hall, p. 99.

Kindred, L. W., D. Bagin and D. R. Gallagher. 1990. *The School and Community Relations.* Englewood Cliffs, N.J.: Prentice Hall, p. 154.

Wood, C. L., E. W. Nicholson and D. G. Findley. 1985. *The Secondary School Principal: Manager and Supervisor.* Boston: Allyn and Bacon, p. 108.

OTHER SUGGESTED READINGS

Baker, C. H. 1985. "Maximizing Mailed Questionnaire Responses," *Image,* 17(4):118–121.

Dillman, D. A. 1978. *Mail and Telephone Surveys: The Total Design Method.* New York: John Wiley and Sons.

Newman, I. 1976. *Basic Procedures in Conducting Survey Research.* Akron, Ohio: The University of Akron.

Sadler, S. 1974. *Survey Techniques for Computer Analysis.* Akron, Ohio: The University of Akron.

Sudman, S. and N. M. Bradburn. 1982. *Asking Questions: A Practical Guide to Questionnaire Design.* San Francisco: Jossey-Bass.

CHAPTER 5

The Personnel Role of the Principal

INTRODUCTION

School principals are very much involved with personnel matters. Some larger school districts have a personnel office at the central administration level with a director of personnel or an assistant superintendent for personnel. The principal who works in such a district should meet with that administrator and review the district's policies and procedures concerning the topics presented in this chapter. However, most school districts are smaller and have no one at the central office in a full-time personnel capacity. In these districts, the superintendent and the school principals share the various personnel responsibilities.

This chapter will discuss the following areas of personnel: forecasting personnel needs, recruiting, interviewing, selecting new teachers, establishing a staff development program, administering the negotiated contract, and disciplining staff members.

FORECASTING PERSONNEL NEEDS

When teachers indicate they are going to resign or retire, some administrators immediately start looking for someone to replace the ones leaving. While that may have been appropriate several decades ago, when enrollment was expanding everywhere and teachers were hard to find, a new approach should be used today.

Each vacant position should be carefully examined by asking these questions:

- Is this position still needed?
- If needed, should it still be full-time?
- Can it be combined with any other position, or some part-time position?

The level the vacancy occurs at makes a difference, too. If you lose a third grade teacher and enrollment is fairly stable, the district will probably have to hire another third grade teacher. However, if a high school English teacher leaves, it may be possible to hire a part-time teacher, say three-fifths or four-fifths, instead of hiring a full-time teacher. The point is that the administration should look at each vacancy and make a conscious decision on how it is to be filled, if at all.

The principal is the administrator who best can assess the future needs of the individual school, knowing the plans for the upcoming year, what changes have taken place in the curriculum and what changes are planned for the future. In addition, the principal knows whether there are going to be organizational changes in the school, whether the student population is increasing, decreasing, or remaining stable, and whether the needs of the student population are changing with regard to needs, course selection (at the high school), or interests. Finally, there may be changes in local or state mandates which affect the number of students who will need the class or course which was taught by the departing teacher. Perhaps the principal can consider the analogy given by Lunenburg and Ornstein (1991). They suggest that principals follow the pattern of basketball coaches who look at their graduating seniors, injured players, and ineligible players and then determine the recruiting needs for the following year, e.g., a point guard. The principal should be equally careful in looking at any vacant position in the school. When all of this has been done, the principal should convey this assessment to the superintendent (or the central office personnel officer) so that he/she can consider the recommendation and start to establish a pool of candidates to fill the vacancy (if that is the decision).

When the assessment is completed and approved, the present job description should be examined to see if it needs to be changed. Bookbinder (1992) states that administrators should not merely describe a job as it presently is or appears to be. Instead, the principal who uses a "human resources planning" approach analyzes "each school's design to determine those specific job requirements that will be required to fulfill the planned school strategy" (p. 140).

RECRUITMENT OF STAFF

Recruitment has been defined as "establishing a pool of potentially acceptable candidates" (Lipham and Hoeh, 1974, p. 236). The first step in recruitment is usually to post (advertise) the position. Depending on the circumstances, vacancies can be posted internally (for the district only) or externally, or both. Circumstances which may affect the posting include wording in the collective bargaining agreement, tradition, the degree to which the district is formal, and the nature of the position itself. For example, it may be more difficult to find a person to teach advanced placement mathematics than it is to find a second grade teacher. This difficulty may influence where the position is advertised.

The job posting should be in writing and circulated to the district staff in some way, either on a bulletin board or in a newsletter. The posting should include the job title, whether it is full- or part-time, a short job description (if necessary), the school where the position will be located, who to apply to for the position, and what is needed from the applicants. For some jobs, a salary or salary range is listed. Posting this job inside the district allows internal candidates to apply for the position, and allows current staff members to recommend others from outside the district to apply. Even if there is no requirement to post jobs, it is good for morale and overall cooperation to post it internally.

While some job vacancies are only posted in the district, others are advertised outside. This is especially necessary in a small district where all vacancies will be filled with new hires. It is also necessary for districts that want to have a larger pool of candidates, especially for hard-to-find positions. Universities with educational placement services can be sent district job vacancies, and asked to include them on their lists of vacancies for students and graduates. School administrators need to plan in advance, since there is a time lag between their posting the position and the university's timetable in making and distributing its listing. If the principal is looking to find an administrative opening, like an assistant principal, there is also the possibility of listing the position in a professional administrative organization's vacancy list or newsletter. State superintendent and principal organizations usually provide this service to their members.

Where else can the principal locate candidates besides universities and professional organizations? Student teachers are an excellent source of candidates since they have been observed on the job by the school's own staff, an opportunity which is usually not available for most candidates. In addition, as mentioned earlier, the current faculty can recommend people who they feel would be an asset to the school. Also, principals and superintendents can obtain recommendations by asking fellow administrators in other districts for names of people who they know are looking for a position. Newspapers should not be overlooked. Candidates do look in the want ads for positions, and administrators will find that they can list positions on short notice for a reasonable cost. Sometimes school officials feel that only noncertificated positions are advertised in newspapers (custodians, cooks, secretaries, etc.), but a glance at most newspapers will reveal notices for teachers, special grant positions, and even administrative positions.

A final word about recruiting from universities – principals should not wait until there is a desperate need in the school to contact the university placement office. They should maintain a relationship with that office even when there are no vacancies. They can drop in to say hello when in the area, give them a call, or drop off some information about the district and the school. The district and each school should update their public relations brochures on a regular basis and use them in recruiting new staff. These should be made available to placement offices each year for their files.

Principals in small, rural areas have some additional problems attracting new people to their schools. Stone (1990) suggests that principals target persons with rural backgrounds, and employ realistic marketing techniques, stressing the real benefits in teaching in rural schools – fewer discipline problems, less red tape, more personal contact, and a greater chance for leadership.

SELECTION OF STAFF

Lipham and Hoeh (1974) define the selection of staff as the "elimination of candidates whose values, interests, needs, and abilities, having been carefully analyzed, fail to satisfy the requirements for a particular role" (p. 236). Once the district has received applications as a result of recruitment efforts, these applications need to be narrowed down, or screened, to a reasonable number for interviews. How this screening is done varies from district to district. Ideally, the district has a set of hiring procedures to define the role that everyone plays in the process – What is the role of the school principal, the department chair or teacher in charge of a grade level, the superintendent, the personnel office (if any)? Are teachers involved in the process? Do administrators interview individually or as a committee? Does the principal make the final selection with the superintendent taking the name to the board for approval, or does the superintendent want to participate in the selection? Obviously, these questions need to be answered by each district in a formal way prior to the actual screening. The procedure, while it may vary from district to district, should not vary from vacancy to vacancy within the same district. For reasons of efficiency, legality, and morality, the same procedures should be followed for every vacancy. Figure 5.1 is an example of hiring procedures developed by one of the authors. It was used, with modifications, in three districts.

Order of Events for a Vacancy
(for a district with a district personnel office)

1. The principal notifies the personnel director that there is a vacancy.
2. The personnel director sends the position to the superintendent to approve for listing or modification.
3. If approved, the position is posted on the vacancy list.
4. The personnel secretary sets up a candidate sheet to list all applicants.
5. The personnel secretary obtains a job description of the position from the principal.
6. The personnel secretary lists the candidates' names on the candidate sheet as they apply.
7. The vacancy list is posted locally and mailed to appropriate persons.
8. Folders are compiled on the candidates.
9. The personnel director and principal identify the interviewers.
10. The personnel secretary issues names and folders to the interviewers. The folders are to remain in the personnel office.
11. After the screening, the personnel director obtains, from the interviewers, the names of all candidates to be interviewed.
12. The personnel secretary arranges the interviews; the screening committee makes reference calls.
13. The committee interviews the candidates and selects, with the principal's approval, a person to be recommended.
14. The personnel director submits the name through the superintendent to the board.
15. Upon approval by the board, the personnel secretary notifies the business office of the new hire.
16. The personnel secretary sends letters to the approved candidate.
17. The personnel secretary sends letters to the candidates not chosen.
18. The personnel secretary files the chosen candidate's folder in the current staff file.
19. The personnel secretary files the other candidate folders in other files, unless on current staff.
20. The personnel director removes the job vacancy from the vacancy list.
21. The personnel secretary files the candidate sheet.

Figure 5.1 *Hiring Procedures.*

Typically, applicants will be asked to submit a letter of application, complete an applicant form, submit a resume, college credentials (references), transcripts, and evidence of the proper state certificate for the position they are seeking. Today, more and more states also require a computer background check by a police department. Some districts will require a test and/or a writing sample from all candidates.

Someone in the district—the personnel office, the principal, a committee, the department chair—must screen the candidates to limit the number for interviews. This is sometimes called a *paper screening* since only the papers of the candidates are seen at this time. It is suggested that more than one person be involved in screening, and that the principal and the department chair (if there is one) be included. The screening committee should keep in mind the vacant position's requirements which were established earlier by the principal and approved by the central administration. Each candidate should be evaluated on how well he or she might fulfill these established needs. A point system might be helpful in determining the final candidates, but a good discussion among the members of the screening committee is even more useful.

When the screening is concluded, one person should call the candidates and tell them they are finalists at this point, ask them if they are still interested (often, some have obtained other jobs), and ask permission to call references and employers to check on their previous employment history. Checking references is one of the most important things that can be done, since past performance is probably the best predictor of future performance. Many administrators leave out this step since it can be time consuming. However, it is not as time consuming as dealing with a new employee who turns out to be incompetent or uncooperative. The time spent on checking references is well worth it.

When the references are checked (and this includes former employers who may not be listed on a reference list by the candidate), the principal (or personnel officer) calls the candidates in for interviews. Lunenburg and Ornstein (1991) state that "despite its widespread use, the interview is a poor predictor of job performance" (p. 473). Kimbrough (1990) agrees that "interviews have been repeatedly found to be an invalid means for selection" (p. 267). Dessler (1988) points out that the interviewer often tends to make a personnel decision during the first few minutes of the interview, then spends the rest of the interview asking questions to obtain information to confirm the decision. Other have said that interviewers often tend to hire people like themselves. Martin (1970) says that schools should have some degree of philosophic disequilibrium in order to foster innovation. Thus, the principal should consider divergent views as he/she interviews candidates, and should not select teachers solely on the basis of their closeness to the principal's views.

Regardless of the opinion that interviews are poor predictors, principals still use them. So, it is appropriate to make some suggestions concerning the interview itself.

It is suggested that a committee be used to interview the candidate. One person will hear what another will miss; one person will ask a question that another would not have asked. It is further suggested, when possible, to have all the candidates interviewed the same day by the same committee. Having an opportunity for a committee to view five candidates in two hours is much better for evaluation that having individual people see the candidates over a period of a week or two. Typically, the committee consists of the principal, assistants (if any), department chair or lead teacher and perhaps someone from the central administration. Maguire (1983) also argues that principals can use teachers to help improve the quality of their selection of other teachers. During these sessions, it is advantageous to keep notes on the interviews and the various responses of the applicants. This will help when it becomes time to compare their responses.

The questions asked in the interview are important and should be established in advance. Although the plan should be to ask each candidate the same questions, allowances must be made for individual questions where appropriate. Some questions are inappropriate to ask any candidate. Don't ask questions about matters that aren't really related to the job and job performance. This rules out such questions as:

- Are you married?
- Do you have children?
- Do you plan to have children?
- Have you ever been arrested?
- What is your husband's (wife's) job?
- Do you have any sons over six feet tall who play basketball? (The authors did not make this one up. One of us heard this question asked during an interview by a board member.)

Some questions which you might want to consider asking are listed in Figure 5.2.

The questions in Figure 5.2 were designed for teacher applicants. Principals will have to ask different questions when interviewing for positions such as custodian and secretary vacancies. However, the same

Tell us about your educational background and experience. (A good beginning to get them talking.)

What do you consider to be your strengths? your weaknesses?

Think of your various teaching (or student teaching, if new teacher) experiences and recall one experience that went very well, maybe better than you expected. Tell me about it.

Tell me about an experience that did not go well. What happened?

What are your future plans? Where do you want to be in five years?

What hobbies and interests do you have outside teaching that give you a chance to relax and do a good job when you return to the classroom?

Why do you want this position?

What do you know about this district? this school?

Why do you want to teach?

While each day is different, imagine that I walked into a typical classroom where you were teaching. What would I see going on? Describe it to me.

Everyone has some disciplinary problems in the classroom. Tell how you handle them.

What grades would you prefer teaching? Why? (If applying for an elementary position; if interviewing for a secondary position, there should be some questions relating to the subject area to test for knowledge, probably asked by the department chair.)

What do you enjoy about teaching?

What questions do you have for us about this position and this school/district? (A candidate should have some questions.)

Think about the best teacher you had. Tell us how that person taught, how they ran the class, what you like and admired. (People often try to teach the way their favorite teacher taught.)

What can you bring to our school?

We are interviewing five people today. Why should we choose you?

Do you have any experience in teaching minorities (or special students or lower level students or older students, etc., depending on the position and the school)?

In our school we are trying (some innovation or new organization). What is your experience with this? Can you adapt to it?

What things have you done successfully to motivate children in the classroom? to establish rapport with them? to get their attention?

How do you work with students with different abilities in the same classroom? What specific things have you done?

What different teaching techniques have you used? Which have been the most successful? Why do you think they worked?

What can I do (as principal, department chair, etc.) to help you?

If I asked the teacher next door to tell me about your teaching, what would he or she say? What would your evaluator say?

What kind of professional books, magazines, or journals do you read?

Why do you want to leave your present job (if employed) for this one?

***Figure 5.2** Interview Questions for Teacher Applicants.*

emphasis should be placed on questions regarding past performance, why they want to come to this new position, and on checking past references and supervisors.

LEGAL ISSUES REGARDING HIRING

In addition to being alert to specific inappropriate or illegal questions, the principal needs to be aware of some federal laws which involve employment discrimination. Discussion on some of these follow.

- *Title VII of the Civil Rights Act of 1964* (later amended)—This law prohibits discrimination in employment (compensation, terms, conditions, or privileges of employment) on the basis of race, religion, color, sex, or national origin. Under these conditions, an employer cannot limit an individual's employment opportunities or affect his status as an employee.
- *Title IX of the Education Amendments of 1972*—This law was originally interpreted to apply only to students, prohibiting, on the basis of sex, the exclusion of a student from participation in any education program or activity receiving financial assistance from the federal government. This law was broadened by Supreme Court decisions in the 1980s to include employees as well as students.
- *Age Discrimination in Employment Act of 1968* (later amended)—This act prohibits discrimination against any person above the age of forty with regard to hiring, firing, and compensating. (Originally, there was an upper age limit in the law. This was removed in 1986.)
- *Vocational Rehabilitation Act of 1973* (later amended)—This law prohibits discrimination against handicapped personnel and requires employers to take affirmative action in hiring and promoting handicapped employees. A stronger measure, the *Americans with Disabilities Act,* was passed by the federal government in 1992.
- *Equal Pay Act of 1963*—This law prohibits wage discrimination on the basis of sex. It requires equal pay for men and women performing the same work.
- *Vietnam Era Veterans Readjustment Act of 1974*—This act requires employers to take affirmative action to employ disabled

Vietnam War veterans and prohibits discrimination against Vietnam War veterans.

- *Pregnancy Discrimination Act of 1978*—This act prohibits discrimination against pregnant women and new mothers in all employment related activities.

In concluding this section, it should be remembered that the interview is only one part of the selection process. Mary Jensen (1987) mentions that teaching is a complex function and that the most capable candidates may not be the ones hired. We need to use as many measures as we can to evaluate the candidates, including high cognitive ability as well as their personal and social skills. Additional information on recruiting, interviewing, and questioning is available from Phi Delta Kappa (William Goldstein, 1986, Bloomington, Indiana).

STAFF DEVELOPMENT AND ORIENTATION

The principal has a responsibility to establish a staff development program for all teachers, and an orientation program for the new teachers. In some districts, the central administration will make plans for one or both of these programs. The principal should have input into the planning of these programs.

Assuming that the principal is left to formulate such a plan, it is suggested that the principal establish a teacher committee to take a needs assessment of the school's faculty. Although some principals impose a staff development program on the faculty (sometimes successfully), it is better to find out what the faculty thinks it needs to learn or to review. A needs assessment of the faculty, carried out by a committee of the teachers themselves, is a good first step to a successful program.

After the assessment has been completed, the teacher committee should meet with the principal and discuss how these needs can best be met in a staff development program. In some cases, outside consultants will have to be brought in, while other needs can be met by having fellow teachers and administrators in the district make the presentations. In most cases, it is better to have an ongoing staff development program during the year to accomplish one or more goals. While there is still a place for the one-shot program or presentation (to accomplish something which can be conveyed in a couple of hours), most staff development goals require the longer, ongoing, year-long program of activities. Also, staff development programs do not have to consist of someone making a speech to the faculty. Sometimes teachers can learn much by visiting other schools, watching a videotape and discussing it in small groups, or by trying simulations and role playing.

The principal must show support to the teacher committee and to the staff development program. Like many things in the school, the responsibility for staff development can be delegated to this committee or to an assistant principal. However, teachers always notice in which areas the principal spends his/her time. If staff development is not one of these areas, the teachers may feel that it is not too important to the principal.

Finally, while this book does not deal with classroom evaluation (part of the instructional role), it is important to point out that the principal may see things during classroom observations which may be appropriate for staff development programs. For example the principal may see deficiencies in classroom discipline, teaching techniques, grouping of students for instruction, etc., that would suggest topics to be considered for the staff development program.

While staff development for the whole faculty is important, this section, in keeping with the earlier discussion on hiring, will emphasize the necessity for having an orientation program for the newly hired teachers in the school. Again, the central administration may take some responsibility for this activity, although the principal must assume some, if not all, of this responsibility.

An orientation is like a first impression. It gives the new teacher a first feeling about the school, how it cares about its teachers, and how much it wants to have the new teacher succeed. Some suggestions follow for an orientation program for new teachers. Some may not be appropriate for every school, but all have been successful at one school or another.

- When a new teacher is hired in the spring or summer, arrange for the local newspaper to send them a short-term subscription. This lets the teacher become acquainted with the community and its activities. The newspaper subscription manager may be willing to do this for free for a potential customer. (One of the authors, as a personnel director, used to send a three-month subscription to new hires. He had received one himself as a new teacher and was really impressed, being able to read about the community several months before moving there.)
- Select an experienced teacher to write to the new teacher to

welcome him or her to the school. This teacher should serve as a mentor to answer questions prior to arrival and when the teacher comes on board. A personal letter from one of the teachers makes a great first impression.

- This should not have to be mentioned – give the teacher the appropriate books, schedules, information about the schools, district, and community, a teacher's manual, and any other material which is available. (Some material is, of course, not available in the spring or summer and will have to be distributed in the fall.)
- Make sure the teacher has met the department chair or lead teacher an has a phone number to reach them prior to the opening of school.
- Give the teacher a tour of the school and, if possible, a tour of the community. Sometimes a real estate agent is very willing to give the community tour since this is a potential client.
- During the first few weeks of school, visit the teacher early and often. Be sure the teacher knows the principal and mentor are available for help and to answer procedural questions as well as inquires such as, "Where do I get more chalk?"
- Make sure the new teacher gets a chance to hear about, and ask questions about, all the record keeping, attendance, and discipline procedures that the school has established. These procedures start on the first day, and cannot wait for a visit from the principal or a first week faculty meeting.
- Introduce the new teacher to the whole staff, to special education personnel, to all administrators in the school, to the secretary and the custodian. The principal should tell the staff to make an extra effort to welcome the new teacher, invite him/her to lunch in the cafeteria, and stop in to say hello during the day. Tell new teachers, or give them a list of who should be contacted for what needs.
- If the school has an orientation day, take the new teachers out to lunch in the community. If possible, invite some community leaders to the lunch to greet the teachers. Tell the teachers about the civic organizations and social clubs available and what the community expects of its schools and its teachers.
- An orientation day for new teachers is a good time to take a tour of the school, where they not only see areas but also can meet

the people who work there. Have the librarians explain their procedures and offerings. Be sure to discuss audiovisual availabilities, and show the computer lab and discuss the scheduling of that room. Tell how teachers order supplies and to whom they take the orders.

- Meet with the new teachers throughout the first semester, not just during the first week. Although the teachers will know where to get the chalk by October, they will have other questions.
- Finally, the principal should talk with the superintendent about putting money into the school budget for orientation and for the staff development program discussed earlier. Although the funding may not be large, its impact will be significant. Even the fact that there is a line item for staff development shows a priority.

CONTRACT ADMINISTRATION

When people think of collective bargaining, they usually think of two sides arguing over money and language, perhaps enduring a strike, and finally reaching an agreement—and the process is over for another year or so. Nothing could be further from the truth for the school principal. Once the contract is approved by both sides, the principal must carry out the provisions of the contract, even though the principal may have been excluded completely from the negotiations process. As Epstein (1974) has stated, "Written agreements negotiated by school boards with teachers and other employees contain a plethora of provisions that many times restrict and reduce the principal's prerogatives. This results from negotiations—in which principals neither participate nor are consulted—that are based on the expediences of reaching settlements rather than the protection of educational effectiveness" (pp. 3–4).

"Thus, the principal is the key member of the management team in contract administration and is the crucial actor in the ongoing drama of living with the provisions of a document that is binding on both parties" (Kaiser, 1985, p. 78).

While principals usually want to cooperate with their teachers and involve them in decision making, they also must realize that they are part of management. As Kaiser points out, there is a difference between providing instructional leadership and being identified personally and professionally with the instructional staff (p. 80).

When the contract is negotiated, it is the responsibility of the central administration to see that all principals know the new contract well. It is suggested that the negotiator, whether an inside or outside person, meet with the administrative staff and go through the new provisions of the contract, giving the principals an opportunity to ask questions about the language and the intent of the language. Only someone who was in attendance at the negotiation sessions can explain the reasons behind the demands and the discussions at the negotiating table.

The principal should be able to administer the contract and represent the administration without displaying antiunion feelings. It is sometimes helpful for the principal to schedule regular meetings with the union's building representative, and not wait until there is a problem. These meetings can help stop problems before they become formal grievances. Also, the principal should keep good records of these discussions and anything related to the contract, including violations of the contract by the teachers. Finally, the principal should assume that the administration can do anything which is not prohibited by the contract (or by law). Often, a teacher will tell a principal, "You cannot do that. There is nothing in the contract that says you can do that." The principal needs to remember that the contract limits what can be done; it does not tell everything that *can* be done.

RESPONDING TO GRIEVANCES

When teachers feel that administration has violated the contract, they sometimes file a formal grievance. These grievances are usually filed at Step 1, the building principal level. Thus, principals need to know how to respond to grievances. While some suggestions are made here, principals should discuss this process with the superintendent or personnel officer of the district before any grievances are filed.

The central administration should designate someone in the central office—the superintendent, personnel officer, chief negotiator—as the contact person for grievances. If the principal receives a grievance, the principal should contact this person immediately. "Since grievances are sometimes filed in different buildings on the same topic, it is important that the administrative response be consistent throughout the district. The central office administrator can advise the principal of other similar grievances, past or present, and discuss appropriate responses'' (Sharp, 1993, p. 113).

When the principal meets with the teacher who filed the grievance, he/she should take notes on the conversation, listen carefully to the arguments put forward, and tell the teacher that he/she will respond in writing to them by the deadline provided in the contract. No response, positive or negative, should be given at this meeting. After the meeting, the principal should contact the central office administrator to discuss the grievance and discuss the response. A copy of the grievance and the principal's response should be sent to the central office.

Many times the grievance stems from some action above the building level, and yet the principal is asked to respond at Step 1. The discussion between the principal and the central office contact person will be very helpful in formulating the principal's response to this grievance. Some general guidelines on grievances are:

- The administration should try to settle at the lowest level, if possible.
- Look at the contract. The grievance should state the exact, specific article and section which is said to have been violated, and should state when it was violated.
- Check to see if the grievance was filed in a timely manner.
- If the grievance involves a new section of the contract, the central office administrator should examine the negotiation notes to see if this problem was discussed during negotiations. These notes may affect the response.
- If the administration decides that it is wrong and the contract has been violated, it may be best to admit to this quickly at the lowest possible level, and settle it before it receives even more attention or goes to arbitration (Sharp, 1993, p. 120).

STAFF DISCIPLINE

One of the principal's managerial duties, and not a pleasant one, is the discipline of staff members. From time to time, various staff members—custodians, cooks, teachers—will do things which are against school policy. As a result, the principal may have to take some action to discipline that staff member.

Before any problems occur, the principal should discuss this topic with

Definition: Examples of minor incidents are tardiness, failure to complete work satisfactorily, an infraction of a rule, policy, procedure or negotiated contract, unprofessional or irresponsible behavior.

1. At the first incident, the principal gives an oral warning and follows this with a written letter to the staff member (see Sample Letter A). A copy of the letter is sent to the superintendent/personnel officer for placement in the staff member's file.

Sample Letter A

On December 5, 19___, you reported to work at 9:00 AM, rather than at 8:00 as required. Since it is important that you come to work on time, we will expect you to arrive no later than 8:00 AM daily. Should you be late again, you may be subject to further disciplinary action.
cc: Superintendent–file

2. For hourly employees who are late to work, the principal follows step 1 at the first incidence and sends Sample Letter B for a repeated violation, with a copy to the superintendent. (District procedures may allow Letter B to be sent initially instead of Letter A.)

Sample Letter B

Due to your late arrival to work on January 10, 19___, you will receive a deduction in your paycheck for the time between your arrival time, 9:00 AM, and the time you were expected for work, 8:00 AM. We expect you to be on time in the future. Any further tardiness may result in further disciplinary action.
cc: Superintendent–file

3. If minor incidents continue, the principal contacts the superintendent to discuss further action, including a short, temporary suspension without pay. The principal should bring supporting documentation to the meeting with the superintendent. The documentation must be accurate, relevant to the incident being discussed, and fairly recent. Any suspension and necessary letters will probably come from the superintendent, depending on district procedures. Sample Letter C can be used by the superintendent.

Sample Letter C

You were late reporting to work on December 4, 6, 8, and 15, 19___. You were sent a warning letter by your principal on each occasion and a copy was made a part of your employment records. In spite of the earlier warnings, you continue to arrive late to work. As a result, you received a pay deduction for your tardiness on December 8. Since you were again late to work on December 15, you are hereby suspended from work, without pay on December 19, 19___, as of 7:00 AM for one day. Any further tardiness will again result in disciplinary action.
cc: personnel file

4. If a similar incident occurs after a suspension, the principal notifies the superintendent to discuss whether another suspension (see Sample Letter D) should take place or whether there are adequate reasons for termination.

Sample Letter D

As enumerated in my letter to you of (date), you have been late to work several times in spite of written warnings, information placed in your permanent file, pay deductions, and a suspension without pay. Because you again have been late to work, on January 9, 19___, you are hereby suspended from work, without pay, on January 16, 17, and 18. Any further tardiness will again result in further disciplinary action.
cc: personnel file

***Figure 5.3** Procedures for Minor Disciplinary Problems.*

the superintendent or district personnel administrator to find out whether the district has established procedures for dealing with this problem. These procedures should be in place. Also, the principal needs to be aware of any negotiated agreements with employee groups which detail procedures for dealing with staff disciplinary problems. Finally, it is helpful for the principal, especially if the principal is new to the district, to see if there are precedents for such action—what was done in the past for various infractions of the rules?

When any incident occurs, the principal needs to keep an accurate written record of the incident, including the date, time, description of the incident, and any witnesses. As stated earlier, the district should have some general guidelines for the principal to follow for the discipline of staff. For principals who do not have such written administrative procedures available to them, Figures 5.3 and 5.4 give some guidance on how to proceed to handle disciplinary problems from the staff.

The examples in Figures 5.3 and 5.4 pertain more to noncertificated staff (custodians, cooks, secretaries, etc.) than to teachers since, in the experience of the authors, more time is spent on discipline of these

Definition: Major incidents include verbal or physical abuse, insubordination, and any act which is seriously detrimental to the school.

1. If a major incident occurs during school hours, the principal contacts the superintendent to discuss possible action. If the incident occurs in the evening, or if it poses an immediate and serious problem, the principal tells the employee to go home and that he/she will be contacted. Then the principal contacts the superintendent.
2. In most cases, where adequate evidence is available, the employee is suspended for a specified amount of time. This is done, with the necessary letters, by the superintendent (see Sample Letter E).

Sample Letter E

On December 11, 19___, you refused a directive from your principal to clean a stairway area at the high school. Because of your refusal to comply with this request and your inadequate responses when questioned about the incident, you are hereby suspended from work, without pay, for three days, December 12–14, 19___. If you wish to discuss this incident with me, please contact my office to set up an appointment. I hope there are no further incidents like this one. Any more will require further disciplinary action, including possible termination.
cc: personnel file

3. The principal and superintendent meet to discuss the incident and past employment history to determine whether a recommendation for termination should be made.

Figure 5.4 *Procedures for Major Disciplinary Problems.*

employees than on teachers. Principals should also note that progressive discipline was used in these procedures. At each increase in the number of incidents, there is a corresponding increase in the penalty. Progressive discipline is important because it demonstrates the willingness of the principal to explain the rule, to give the person a second chance (for minor incidents), and to make the severity of the penalty fit the incident.

It is important to give the employee his/her due process rights, and any rights and procedures outlined in a negotiated agreement. The employee should know what the problem is. He or she should be told about any supporting evidence, and should be allowed to respond to the accusations. The principal, if not directly involved, should investigate any incident to be sure of all of the facts. Finally, the employee has the right of appeal to the superintendent and to the board of education.

SUMMARY

This chapter discussed the role of the principal in personnel. Recognizing that the central office must establish certain procedures and may have a full-time personnel officer, this chapter presented certain topics which are relevant to most principals: forecasting personnel needs in the schools, recruiting and selecting personnel, establishing a staff development program, administering the negotiated contract, and disciplining staff members. The next chapter will present some examples from school case law that involve cases similar to those encountered by the building principal.

THE PRINCIPAL'S CASEBOOK

The Case of the Curious Candidates

You and your screening committee complete their work and narrow the teaching vacancy candidates down to four people. Two problems come up: (1) one of your teachers comes into your office and announces that she knows a terrific candidate (who is not in your original pool) who "just happens to be out in my car." (2) One of the screening committee members reports to you that reference calls on the finalists revealed that one candidate had great references from one school and questionable ones from another school. The person giving the negative references has not had his contract renewed.

Questions to Consider

- What do you tell your teacher (with her friend outside)?
- Do you increase the finalists at this point?
- Do you miss a chance to get a "terrific" teacher in order to follow procedures?
- Which reference check do you believe?
- What should you do now about that candidate?

REFERENCES

Bookbinder, R. M. 1992. *The Principal: Leadership for the Effective and Productive School.* Springfield, IL: Charles C. Thomas, Publisher.

Dessler, G. 1988. *Personnel Management.* Englewood Cliffs, N.J. Prentice-Hall.

Epstein, B. 1969. *Principals: An Organized Force for Leadership.* Reston, VA: National Association of Secondary School Principals.

Goldstein, W. 1986. *Recruiting Superior Teachers: The Interview Process.* Bloomington, IN: Phi Delta Kappa

Jensen M. 1987. *How to Recruit, Select, Induct, and Retain the Very Best Teachers.* Eugene, OR: ERIC Clearinghouse.

Kaiser, J. S. 1985. *The Principalship.* Minneapolis, MN: Burgess Publishing Co.

Kimbrough, R. B. and C. W. Burkett. 1990. *The Principalship: Concepts and Practices.* Englewood Cliffs, N.J.: Prentice-Hall, Inc.

Lipham, J. M. and J. A. Hoeh. 1974. *The Principalship: Foundations and Functions.* New York: Harper and Row.

Lunenburg, F. C. and A. C. Ornstein. 1991. *Educational Administration: Concepts and Practices.* Belmont, CA: Wadsworth Publishing Co.

Maguire, J. 1983. "Faculty Participation in Interviewing Teacher Candidates," *The Clearing House,* 56 (7): 330–331.

Martin, W. M. 1970. "Role Conflict and Deviant Adaptation as Related to Educational Goal Attainment: A Social Systems Approach," Ph.D. diss., University of California, Los Angeles.

Sharp, W. L. 1993. *Collective Bargaining in the Public Schools.* Madison, WI: Wm. C. Brown Publishers

Stone, D. 1990. "Recruiting and Retaining Teachers in Rural Schools," *Far West Laboratory Knowledge Brief.* San Francisco, CA: Far West Lab.

CHAPTER 6

School Law for Principals

INTRODUCTION

Although it may be of great interest to the federal government, the primary responsibility for education rests with the fifty state governments. The word "education" is not mentioned anywhere in the United States Constitution. The Tenth Amendment has been interpreted to say that education is reserved to the individual states. This amendment reads as follows:

> The powers not delegated to the United States by the Constitution, nor prohibited by it to the States, are reserved to the States respectively, or to the people.

Thus, the responsibility for education rests in the state legislatures. These bodies have the legal authority to establish the kind of educational organization they desire. With the exception of Hawaii, which has only one school district, the state legislatures have chosen to establish local boards of education, and delegate to them certain powers such as hiring a superintendent, establishing local policies, and supervising the running of the school through the superintendents and principals which they hire.

There are two legal concepts which are important to this chapter—*in loco parentis* and *governmental immunity.* Historically, school personnel have stood "in the place of the parents" (in loco parentis) in their dealings with school discipline. As an example, the Illinois School Code (Section 24-24, 1992) states: "In all matters relating to the discipline in and conduct of the schools and the school children, they [teachers and other certificated employees] stand in the relation of parents and guardians to the pupils. This relationship shall extend to all activities connected with the school program, including all athletic and extracurricular programs, and may be exercised at any time for the safety and supervision of the pupils in the absence of their parents or guardians."

The in loco parentis concept was weakened in the late 1960s and early 1970s by court decisions like *Tinker* (explained later) and by laws such as the Family Educational Rights and Privacy Act (P.L. 93-380, 1974) which allows parents to see the educational records of their children.

Governmental immunity, like in loco parentis, has also been affected by the courts. Governmental immunity comes from the English concept of sovereign immunity, simply stated, "The king can do no wrong." This concept was abolished in England in 1890. In 1959, an Illinois case, *Molitor* (full citation listed at end of chapter), resulted in a decision that a person can collect damages from a school district. Peter Molitor, a student in an Illinois public school, was severely injured when his school bus ran off the road and exploded. The Illinois Supreme Court ruled against the traditional concept of governmental immunity and awarded damages. These two concepts will play a role in several of the cases discussed in this chapter dealing with the issues of religion in the schools, student rights, discrimination, searches, torts, academic freedom, and the principal's role in these issues.

RELIGIOUS ISSUES IN THE SCHOOLS

The First Amendment of the Constitution says:

> Congress shall make no law respecting an establishment of religion, or prohibiting the free exercise thereof; of abridging the freedom of speech, or of the press; or the right of the people peaceably to assemble, and to petition the Government for a redress of grievances.

Many activities which were commonplace in schools have been declared in violation of the establishment clause of the First Amendment. Principals should note the following cases as examples of those activities which are no longer appropriate.

McCollum—Religious teachers came into the public schools weekly during regular school hours to teach religion for a short period of time. The Supreme Court ruled that tax-supported schools cannot side with religious groups to help them spread their faith.

Abington—The school in this case required the daily reading of the *Bible,* excusing those students who did not wish to participate. A similar case, *Murray* decided at the same time, involved the recitation of the Lord's Prayer. In both cases, the Supreme Court stated that the First Amendment was being violated. Principals should note that making the activities voluntary did not make them constitutional. The *Bible,* however, can be studied in schools as literature.

Engle—The Supreme Court ruled that public schools could not use prayers in schools even though the prayer used in this case was nonsectarian, and participation by students was voluntary. A 1992 decision ruled that prayers and benedictions at public school graduation ceremonies—which probably extends to ball games, pep rallies, or any other school activities—were in violation.

Stone—In Kentucky, a copy of the Ten Commandments was provided through private funds to be placed on the walls of each classroom in the public schools. Again, the Supreme Court ruled that this was plainly religious in nature and served no educational function. It violated the establishment clause of the First Amendment.

STUDENT RIGHTS

Historically, students were not regarded as people with constitutional rights. Using the in loco parentis concept, school administrators often felt they had all the rights the parents of the students had. The freedom to dress as they liked, speak as they liked, or write what they liked stopped when students entered the school building. In a case which was not related to school *(In re Gault)*, a court ruled that children, as well as adults, were entitled to due process. This led to the famous Tinker case.

Tinker—John Tinker and some other students wore black armbands to show their objections to the war in Vietnam. The principal, hearing that this might happen, issued a statement that no student could wear such an armband. When they did, he suspended the students. The Supreme Court ruled that the armband was a symbolic act covered by the First Amendment and is related to pure speech. The Court stated the language which has been quoted often since the decision, that neither "students or teachers shed their constitutional rights to freedom of speech or expression at the school house gate." Thus, the principal has to balance the constitutional rights of the individual student with the obligation to protect the other students, and to maintain an efficient and orderly school system.

Gambino—A principal ordered a student not to publish an issue of the student newspaper because the principal objected to an article in that issue. A federal district court ruled that the paper was protected by the

First Amendment as a vehicle for student expression and could not be regulated by the administration. On the other hand, a decision in Williams said that an issue of a paper could be stopped when it had an ad for drug paraphernalia. The federal court of appeals ruled that the health and safety of the students override the First Amendment rights of students.

Due process for students is an important concept which will be discussed in Chapter 8, which covers student discipline. This concept comes from the *Gault* and *Tinker* decisions and from the Fourteenth Amendment (detailed in Chapter 8). Another decision, based on the Fourteenth Amendment, concerns right of students to object to saluting the flag.

Barnette—A state law in West Virginia said that all students and teachers were required to salute the flag daily and recite the pledge of allegiance. The Supreme Court ruled that no official can prescribe what is orthodox in politics and require others to follow that prescription.

DISCRIMINATION

The previous chapter on personnel mentioned several areas to watch to avoid discrimination, such as recruiting, selecting and hiring staff. One of the laws mentioned, Title IX, applies to students. This law prohibits discrimination based on gender in educational programs. Specifically, it prohibits the separation of students by sex in such programs as physical education, industrial arts and home economics. Most of the publicity regarding implementation of this law in public schools revolves around athletics. The law does recognize that there can be separation in sports where contact with those on competing teams is required. But there have been legal challenges on contact sports. Principals should realize that both sexes require equal treatment by the administration in terms of practice times, facilities, budgets, and travel. Here are some guidelines written by Fischer and Schimmel (1982):

(1) If team competition is available for boys, it should also be available for girls.
(2) In noncontact sports, if there is no team for girls, they may compete for positions on the boys' team.
(3) If there are teams for both, courts tend to respect the separation of the sexes for athletic activities (p. 274).

SEARCHES

Principals are sometimes confronted with the possibility of drugs or weapons being hidden in a student locker or on the student. Whether a search can be made stems from the Fourth Amendment and the court cases involving the amendment:

> The right of the people to be secure in their persons, houses, papers, and effects, against unreasonable searches and seizures, shall not be violated, and no Warrants shall issue, but upon probable cause, supported by Oath or affirmation, and particularly describing the place to be searched, and the persons or things to be seized.

Overton—In this locker search case, police obtained a search warrant and searched a student locker, looking for drugs. A court of appeals stated that the school retains the control of the lockers and has the power to search a locker because of the special relationship that administrators have with students. In fact, the court said the administrator has a duty to inspect when there is suspicion of something illegal.

T.L.O.—A female student (T.L.O.) was suspected of smoking in the school restroom. She said that she did not smoke at all. The assistant vice-principal asked to see her purse and discovered cigarettes, rolling papers, marijuana, a pipe, money, a list of students who owed her money, and two letters that implicated her in dealing drugs. The Supreme Court said that schools do not have to have a search warrant, nor does the search have to be based on probable cause, but on the reasonableness of the search, under all circumstances.

The Fourth Amendment does not prohibit searches. It prohibits *unreasonable* searches. Sufficient probability, not certainty, is the "touchstone of reasonableness." The administrator, in this case, had a reasonable suspicion that T.L.O.'s purse would have cigarettes in it. In other words, school administrators are subject to a lower standard for searches than are police officers, since administrators still have an in loco parentis function. While the police must have *probable cause,* the school administrator only needs *reasonable suspicion.* Principals can search lockers and clothing in order to maintain an orderly educational atmosphere in the school building. In fact, as the court said, it could be argued that the principal has an obligation to search for drugs and weapons, when the principal suspects they exist, in order to protect the health and welfare of the students.

Certain searches should be avoided. Strip searches of students and using dogs to detect drugs on students have been ruled as too intrusive. Dog searches of lockers and automobiles have been allowed by the courts.

Some guidelines for searches are:

(1) The search is based on reasonable grounds for believing that something contrary to school rules, or significantly detrimental to the school and its students, will be found in the locker.
(2) The information leading to the search and seizure is independent of the police.
(3) The primary purpose of the search is to secure evidence of student misconduct for disciplinary purposes, although it may be contemplated that in appropriate circumstances the evidence would also be made available to the police. If evidence of a crime or grounds for a juvenile proceeding is lawfully obtained by school personnel, it may be turned over to police and used by them.
(4) The school has keys or combinations to the lockers, and the students are on some form of prior notice that the school reserves the right to search the lockers (Olson, 1971, pp. 49–50).

McCarthy and Cambron (1981) suggest:

(1) A search warrant must be obtained if police officials are conducting a search.
(2) Both students and parents should be informed that searches can and will be conducted when necessary.
(3) Before a search is ever conducted, school personnel should ask the students to volunteer any evidence of contraband in their possession.
(4) The person conducting the search should do so in the presence of another staff member.
(5) There should be absolutely no strip searches or mass searches.
(6) All searches should be based upon reasonable belief that some illegal material is present (pp. 307–308).

TORT LIABILITY

A tort is a civil wrong (not contractual) that results in some injury for which the court may reward damages. The most common tort injury is negligence. As stated previously, schools are no longer protected by governmental immunity, and school personnel can be charged with negligence. There are usually two tests applied to see if a staff member is negligent. First, staff members can be found negligent if they do not act in a reasonable manner. This is defined as acting as a reasonably prudent person would act under the same circumstances. The second test is foreseeability. Could the staff member have foreseen and/or prevented the circumstances which led to the injury? The *Wilkinson* case, discussed in full in Chapter 3, is an example of a tort that was successful because the board of education knew about the possibility of someone getting injured by the glass in the gymnasium foyer, since someone else had been hurt there earlier. They could have *foreseen* the possibility for further injury. Also, their action (or, rather, inaction) in not fixing the problem was not a *reasonable* response under the circumstances. Below is another case which shows that the courts can also be reasonable in issuing judgements.

Fagan—During a recess, a student threw a small rock, found on the playground, which bounced against a larger stone and hit a boy (Fagan) in the eye, causing the loss of the eye. Fagan's parents felt that the school should have kept the playground in better shape and provided more supervision. The Wyoming state supreme court ruled for the school, stating that there is no requirement for the supervising teacher to have under constant scrutiny all precise spots of play. Supervision does not have to be continuous and direct at all times in all places on the playground. Finally, just the fact there were rocks on the playground does not make it a dangerous and defective condition. In short, the actions of the supervisor had been reasonable, and she could not have foreseen that the rock would hit a second rock and strike the boy.

The *Fagan* case does point out the necessity for the principal to be sure that all areas are properly supervised, especially those areas which can be problem areas—science labs, playgrounds, home economics and industrial arts rooms, athletic fields and gyms. These areas must be properly supervised and have equipment which is in good shape. Also, students must be properly trained to use the equipment in these areas. One of the authors had an industrial arts student who was severely injured when he cut his hand on a machine. When the incident was investigated, it was found that not only did the student get training on the machine, he had to take a test on the machine before using it and had scored a perfect score on the exam. This gave the school evidence that the student had been adequately trained. As a result, no law suit was filed.

What can be done to reduce the possibility of tort liability? The building walk-through described in Chapter 3 is a good way to begin to examine the building on a regular basis. In addition, the National Association of Secondary School Principals has made some suggestions for reducing liability. These guidelines are:

(1) The exercise of due care requires an administrator to attempt to foresee dangers to students in his or her charge and to take whatever precautions seem reasonable to avoid them.
(2) Specifically, an administrator is expected to establish rules for the guidance of his or her staff and to assign adequate supervision for any student activity, but the school and its staff are not expected to be an insurer of the health and safety of their students.
(3) The greater the possibility of injury, the greater the efforts which should be made to assure student safety.
(4) The closer the relationship of a student activity to the purposes and educational program of the school, the more likely a principal or other administrator is to be held accountable to the students for their well being.
(5) In circumstances where supervision and control of student welfare is unfeasible, extra care should be taken to assure that the circumstances into which the student is placed are not fraught with inherent dangers. Any necessary risks should be brought to the attention of both the student and his or her parents in advance.
(6) The degree of care required and the consequent amount of supervision expected increases as the age and maturity of the students involved decrease.
(7) The location in which a student is injured is only one factor in the consideration of whether there was negligence and consequent legal liability on the part of a principal or other educator (NASSP, 1975).

ACADEMIC FREEDOM

The state legislatures have given school boards broad powers to establish educational programs within the parameters of the state mandates. Likewise, the courts have given the schools wide discretion in carrying out these programs that they have established. Thus, when parents have questioned the right of the board to establish certain programs and courses, the courts have generally sided with the schools. However, once the curriculum has been established by the board of education, there still have been challenges dealing with academic freedom. Following are two cases involving different aspects of this concept.

Keefe—A teacher was suspended with the possibility of being fired after he gave seniors a reading assignment in *Atlantic Monthly* which contained a "vulgar" word. Students were allowed to choose an alternate assignment if they wished. The court sided with the teacher, finding the article scholarly, and stating that the parents' sensibilities were not the full measure of what is education. The court objected to the "chilling effect" of the censorship (a phrase often seen in these opinions).

Pico—A school board attended a conference and obtained a list of books which were said to be objectionable. After some study, the board ordered that those titles in their school libraries be removed. The court said that the books had to be returned to the library because the Constitution does not permit the official suppression of ideas. While the board has the right to select the books in the first place, it cannot remove them from the library after they have been placed there.

To conclude this chapter, principals are urged to learn what the state law (school code) says, and what is stated in the district's school board policy manual and in administrative procedures. For example, it does not help to know all about student due process and court decisions affecting the administering of corporal punishment if the principal does not realize that the district board policy prohibits it. Also, most state and national principal associations try to keep their members informed about recent court decisions that could affect them. Principals should note these articles in their professional journals and newsletters. Finally, principals should not hesitate to ask the superintendent or personnel office for advice. Districts need to be consistent in their dealing with students and staff, and good communications from individual principals to the central office will help. Principals and superintendents need to remember that they are not attorneys, and may need to contact their law firms for advice.

SUMMARY

This chapter discussed the principal's role with respect to school law. Specifically, it covered the areas of religion in the schools, student rights, discrimination, searches of lockers and students, torts, and academic freedom. Due process for students will be discussed in the chapter on student discipline. The next chapter looks at the food service program in the school and gives suggestions for the principal for dealing with this program.

THE PRINCIPAL'S CASEBOOK

The Case of the Sliding Student

You have just received a phone call from a parent of one of your high school students. She stated that her daughter had been injured in physical education class, which was news to you. Sue, the daughter, was on a team playing a game which the instructor called "sliding." The students in this game were supposed to lie on their stomachs on a small sled, with wheels, and push themselves around the gymnasium floor. To you, it sounded something like a soccer or hockey game. Anyway, during this game, Sue was pushed against the side of the gym where the teacher had placed long boards to keep the ball in play. The loose board hit Sue in the head and caused her to go to the hospital for treatment.

Questions to Consider

- Do you understand the game or do you need to ask the teacher to explain it to you?
- Do you have any opinion about the equipment—the sled and the boards?
- Is there negligence involved? If so, who is negligent?
- Do you need to contact the attorney? the insurance company? Why would you call the insurance company?
- What do you think about this activity, apart from any injury?
- What would you tell Sue's mother on the phone?
- What would you do after the phone call?

REFERENCES*

Abington. *School Dist. of Abington Twp.* v. *Schempp,* 374 U.S. 203, 83 S.Ct. 1560. (1963).

*Case law references are listed alphabetically according to the terms used in the text, even though that term may be the second party in the case.

Barnette. *West Virginia St. Bd. of Ed.* v. *Barnette,* 319 U.S. 624, 63 S. Ct. 1178 (1943).

Engle. *Engle* v. *Vitale,* 370 U.S. 421, 82 S. Ct. 1261 (1962).

Fagan. *Fagan* v. *Summers,* Sup. Ct. of Wyoming, 498 P. 2d 1227 (1972).

Fischer, L. and D. Schimmel. 1982. *The Rights of Students and Teachers.* New York: Harper and Row.

Gambino. *Gambino* v. *Fairfax City Sch. Bd.* 429 F. Supp. 731, 734 (1977).

Illinois School Code, 1992. St. Paul, Minn.: West Publishing Co.

In re Gault, 387 U.S. 1 Ariz. (1967).

Keefe. *Keefe* v. *Geanakos,* U.S. Ct. of Appeals, 1st, 418, F. 2d 359 (1969).

McCarthy, M. M. and N. H. Cambron. 1981. *Public School Law: Teachers' and Students' Rights.* Boston: Allyn and Bacon.

McCollum. *People of Illinois, McCollum* v. *Bd. of Ed., Champaign,* 333 U.S. 203, 68 S. Ct. 461 (1948).

Molitor. *Molitor* v. *Kaneland Comm. Unit Dist. 302,* 18 ILL. 2d 11, 163 N.E. 2d 89 (1959).

Murray. *Murray* v. *Curlett,* same citation as Abington case.

National Association of Secondary School Principals. 1975. "A Legal Memorandum. Responsibilities for Student Injury Occurring off School Property," Reston, VA: NASSP, March–April.

Olson, E. 1971. "Student Rights–Locker Searches," *NASSP Bulletin,* (February):55.

Overton. *People* v. *Overton,* 20 N.Y. 2d 360, 283 N.Y. S. 2d 22, 229 N.E. 2d 596, (1967), affirmed on reargument 24 N.Y. 2d 522, 301 N.Y. S. 2d 479, 249 N.E. 2d 366 (1969).

Pico. *Bd. of Ed., Island Trees Union Free Sch. Dist. 26* v. *Pico,* 457 U.S. 853, 102 S. Ct. 2799 (1982).

Stone. *Stone* v. *Graham,* 449 U.S. 39, 101 S. Ct. 192 (1980).

Tinker. *Tinker* v. *Des Moines Indep. Comm. Sch. Dist.,* 393 U.S. 503, 89 S. Ct. 733 (1969).

T.L.O. *New Jersey v. T.L.O.,* U.S. 325, 105 S. Ct. 733 (1985).

United States Constitution.

Wilkinson. *Wilkinson* v. *Hartford Accident Co.,* 411 So. 2d 22 (1982).

Williams. *Williams* v. *Spencer,* 622 F. 2d 1200 (1980).

CHAPTER 7

The Principal and Food Service

INTRODUCTION

Nearly every principal is forced to deal on some level with food service. Just as the neighborhood red brick elementary school is all but a memory, so are the hour-long lunches that teachers and students once knew. And, for those old red brick buildings that have managed to escape the wrecker's ball, the basements, gyms, assembly halls and even classrooms have become makeshift cafeteria spaces.

The principal is either involved in a cafeteria program housed in the building, a satellite program with food sent from a central location, or with an outside food service that serves the district. Whichever is the case, the principal will have input, because such operations are a part of the school and, as such, are under the principal's jurisdiction.

As the person responsible for the building, the principal should at least understand the basics of the food service program. Often, this area will become a bone of contention with students, parents, and even with the teachers.

This chapter discusses the following areas: the school lunch, line and staff relationships, leftover food, safety and sanitation guidelines, and some job descriptions for the food service staff. Unlike the text of some of the other chapters in this book, this chapter contains several lists of standards for the cafeteria, especially in the safety/sanitation areas. The purpose of providing these lists is to give the principal a resource to which he/she can refer to check the quality of the cafeteria.

THE SCHOOL LUNCH

What are the components of the typical school lunch (formerly called the Class A lunch)?

Can there be substitutions?

Can the principal initiate offerings that go beyond the set program?

According to the United States Department of Agriculture (USDA), the nutritional goal of the typical lunch is to furnish at least a third of the recommended daily dietary allowance for children ages six to eighteen.

A typical lunch, as specified in the *USDA Regulations*, shall contain as a minimum each of the following food components:

(1) *Meat and meat alternate*–Two ounces (edible portion as served) of lean meat, poultry, or fish; or two ounces of cheese; or one egg; or one-half cup of any combination of the above-listed foods. To be counted in meeting this requirement, these foods must be served in a main dish and one other menu item.

(2) *Vegetables and fruits*–Three-fourths cup serving consisting of two or more vegetables or fruits or both. A serving of full-strength vegetable or fruit juice may be counted to meet not more than half this requirement.

(3) *Bread*–Eight servings per week of whole grain or enriched bread or other breads such as corn bread, biscuits, rolls, muffins, made of whole grain or enriched meal or flours (or, as an alternative, pasta). There must be at least one serving per day.

(4) *Fluid milk*–One-half pint of fluid milk as a beverage. A choice must be offered; the milk served must be a choice of whole milk and a form of low-fat plain milk.

Someone once said, " 'Class A' doesn't necessarily mean classy." Sometimes, these typical lunches lose their appeal. In all fairness to the cafeteria cooks, one can only do so much with government commodities. It is the wise principal who will initiate other options for the customers of the cafeteria.

A salad bar is certainly a nice addition that will whet the appetite of adults and teens alike. Weight-conscious students will appreciate the greens and the crispy vegetables. The salad bar is thrifty, too, because the vegetables can be recycled into soups.

Another excellent idea is to establish a build-your-own-baked-potato bar. There can be a charge for the potato and for each additional topping.

Adults and students both enjoy soup and sandwiches. Let them have a couple of choices, and they will think they are dining at a restaurant. Another suggestion is to ask the cooks to come up with a quarter-pound hamburger and name it after the school's mascot—the Mustang Burger or the Lancer Burger, etc. These can be served on ball game days. Free and reduced lunch customers will have to maintain the Class A lunch so that the school can collect government dollars.

LINE AND STAFF

Where does the building principal generally fit into the food service program?

Figure 7.1 shows a typical schematic for line and staff. One aspect listed is a food service advisory committee. The principal needs input from members of the district as well as from students. By having such a committee, the principal is in better standing with the foods division of the local state department of education.

LEFTOVER FOOD

What happens to leftover food?
To whom does it belong?

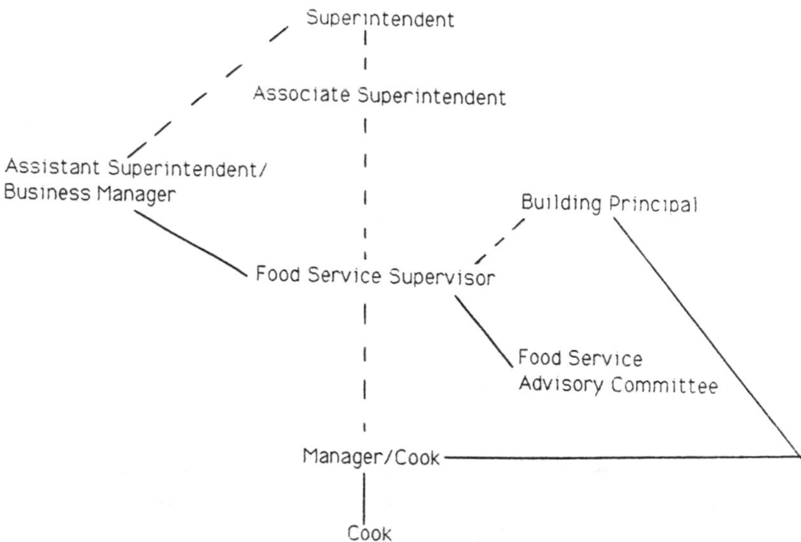

Figure 7.1 *Line and Staff Chart. (Note: the number and position of the people on this chart will vary with the size of the school district. This is just one possibility.)*

A principal who has been on the job for any length of time will come across these questions, and there is only one correct answer—the school. Cooks, cafeteria workers, and other staff members cannot be allowed to take home leftovers without paying for them. The cafeteria staff should not make extra food so that there will be food for them to take home, paid for or not. If there is food which would otherwise go to waste, the cooks can purchase this food at the regular adult price. The smart principal can address the situation by posting the following sign in several conspicuous locations in the cafeteria kitchen:

> All food consumed by Food Services employees is to be *paid* for at the appropriate *Adult Price.* Leftovers, runouts, specials, etc., are *not* to be given away or sold to employees for less than they were priced to adults. All food should be paid for prior to consumption.

The cautious principal should periodically check the cooks' packages and see if they have a receipt for any food being taken out. Toast, butter, jelly, and coffee are often consumed by cafeteria cooks with no thought of paying for them. These items are not perks, and the costs must be borne by the consumers. The principal should check before lunch starts, too, and make certain that the cafeteria manager gives receipts for food purchased. If the principal asks to see a receipt, he/she is showing fiscal stewardship that is expected of an executive. The principal should be sure to pay for all items consumed personally and should let the cafeteria staff know from the outset that he/she has the same expectations from them. If the principal finds the staff either taking home leftovers without paying for them, or eating breakfasts or lunches for free, the principal should handle the situation with progressive discipline as described in Chapter 5—a verbal warning, a written letter, a suspension, possible termination. Stealing is stealing. The food has been purchased with taxpayers money, either directly or through the government. As the saying goes, "There is no such thing as a free lunch."

SAFETY AND SANITATION GUIDELINES

The principal is responsible for the safety and well-being of food service employees, students, and staff. The principal should have a say in the dress code, the work habits (as they pertain to safety and sanitation), as well as food protection and preparation.

The following guidelines outline sanitation practices that need to be followed in any food service operation in order to protect the health of the customers. Also included are safety guidelines designed to protect the health and well-being of the employee. Because of their importance, each food service employee should have a working knowledge of these guidelines. The first part of this section addresses the employee; the second part addresses food protection.

The Food Service Employee

A. Personal Appearance
   The personal appearance of the employee is important for sanitation and safety reasons, as well as for the impression the employee gives of the cafeteria operations.
   1. Shoes
      The employee's shoes must be complete (no open toes or heels), comfortable to wear, provide support, and provide protection from heavy or sharp objects that may fall upon the feet. The soles should be made of a substance that will grip the floor to prevent falls from slippery floors. Shoes should be kept clean, polished, and in good repair.
   2. Jewelry
      Wedding rings, engagement rings, and button type earrings for pierced ears are acceptable. Dangling earrings, clip-on earrings, pins, necklaces, etc., are not to be worn in the kitchen while working.
   3. Personal Hygiene
      Employees must bath daily, use a deodorant, and brush their teeth with a dentifrice. Conservative use of makeup and perfume is acceptable. Fingernail polish or false fingernails are not permitted, as they can chip into the food.
   4. Storage of Personal Items
      All coats, purses, sweaters, and other personal items should be kept in the lockers provided, or in a designated place assigned by the Manager/Cook. At no time should articles of clothing be hanging on equipment, storage racks or left anywhere the clothing can come in contact with food-contact surfaces or equipment. Lockers should be kept locked to prevent loss of personal items. Employees must provide their own locks (the combination or the spare key must be on file in the manager/cook's office).

The principal of the building needs to periodically check to see that these basic rules of sanitation are being met. Inappropriate dress or lack of hygiene should be dealt with by the manager/cook.

B. Health of Employee
No person while affected with a disease in a communicable form, or while a carrier of such a disease, or while afflicted with boils, infected wounds, a cold, diarrhea, gastrointestinal upsets, or a respiratory infection can work in school food service. Employees with such health problems must immediately notify the manager/cook.
  1. Cuts
  Persons with cuts that are not infected may work provided the cut is completely bandaged and a guard cover is used.

C. Employee Work Habits
In order for good sanitation and safety procedures to be effective, they must be practiced at all times. Good sanitation and safety procedures must be developed in the work habits of the employee.
  1. Washing of Hands
  Hands are to be washed in the sink provided for this purpose, with soap and warm water, never in the sink where food is being prepared. Hands should be washed:
    a. after arriving and before starting work
    b. after eating
    c. after handling soiled equipment
    d. after blowing nose, sneezing, or coughing
    e. after combing hair or arranging hair
    f. after coffee breaks
    g. after handling money
    h. as needed
  2. Dish Towels
  Cooks should wipe their hands, face, and/or arms with paper towels and never with a dish towel. Dishes and equipment should be air-dried and not dried with a towel. If dish towels are used for cleaning surfaces and equipment and are dropped on the floor, they should not be used again until washed.
  3. Eating Drinking, and Smoking
    a. Food should only be eaten in the dining room during assigned breaks or lunch period.

   b. If an employee is thirsty, the cook should go to the water fountain for a drink or get a glass of water, drink it, and return the glass to the soiled dish area. Cooks should not keep a glass of liquid in the work area for sipping.

4. Tasting

   Tasting is a very important part of a cook's job. Food must be tasted in order to judge quality. The cook should use a clean spoon (not a finger) for tasting, and the spoon should not be reused.

Again, the principal needs to do periodic walk-throughs to be certain these guidelines and rules are followed. The principal should remember that if a sanitation inspector or a food service division inspector from the state department of education visits, the principal has a responsibility for seeing that these guidelines are met.

Some other important matters for the principal to check:

5. Work Surfaces
   a. Dirty dishes, pots, and boxes should not be placed on a food preparation work surface.
   b. Cooks should not lean or sit on food preparation work surfaces.
   c. These food preparation work and wall surfaces must be kept clean at all times.
6. Handling Equipment and Utensils
   a. Cooks should be alert to any utensil not properly washed.
   b. They should set aside any chipped or cracked equipment.
   c. Cooks should not use any equipment or utensil that falls on the floor.
   d. The staff should keep fingers away from the rim of glasses, the eating end of silverware, and the food contact surface of the plate.
7. Serving Food
   a. If a serving utensil falls into the food, another one should be used to get it out.
   b. Equipment should be used to serve or prepare food, not the hands (unless covered with a hand guard).

Following are some safety procedures which principals should know. If the staff follows these procedures, worker's compensation claims for the kitchen may be reduced.

8. Safety Procedures
   a. Slicing should be done away from the body, not toward the body.
   b. Knives, two-pronged forks, and other sharp tools should be stored in special areas.
   c. Such sharp tools should not be covered with a cloth or towel on a table.
   d. If one of these tools is dropped, it should be left to fall. The cook should not attempt to catch it.
   e. Safety guards should be used on meat slicers.
   f. People using equipment should be trained for its use and should know the safety procedures for its use.
   g. Broken china and glassware should be cleaned up immediately, using a broom and dust pan. Place broken pieces in a special container.
   h. Cutting knives should not be placed with dirty pots and pans for cleaning.
   i. Clean any liquid spills from the floor immediately.

Food Protection

In order to avoid having the school shut down by food poisoning or other food-related epidemics, cafeteria staff should follow these basic principles.

A. General Goal
   All food, while being stored, prepared, served, or sold in the cafeteria, or transported from the cafeteria, should be protected against contamination from dust, insecticides, flies, rodents, and other vermin; unclean utensils and work surfaces; unnecessary handling; coughing and sneezing; flooding, drainage, and overhead leakage; and any other source of contamination.
B. Temperatures
   1. Each facility used for the storage of potentially hazardous food must have a thermometer located in the warmest part of the facility in which the food is stored.
   2. All perishable food should be stored at temperatures that will protect against spoilage.
   3. All potentially hazardous food should be maintained at a safe temperature (45°F or below; at 140°F or above) except during

the necessary minimum periods of actual preparation and serving.

4. All hot foods should be served at a temperature of 165°F or higher.
5. Frozen food should be stored at or below 0°F. Frozen food should be thawed by placing it in a refrigerator at 45°F or below until thawed as part of the continuous cooking process, or thawed by any other method which has been approved by the health department as safe and satisfactory.

C. Preparation

1. When using utensils such as forks, tongs, and spoons for preparation, the handle portion of the utensil should not come in contact with the food.
2. All raw fruits and vegetables should be washed thoroughly before being cooked or served.
3. Fresh pork, stuffings, poultry, and stuffed meats/poultry should be heated to a minimum temperature of 165°F throughout.
4. Meat salads, poultry salads, potato salads, egg salads, cream-filled pastries, and other potentially hazardous processed foods should be prepared from chilled products, with a minimum of manual contact, and on surfaces and with utensils which are clean and which have been sanitized prior to use.

D. Storage

1. All food items and nonfood items must be stored away from cleaning and chemical supplies.
2. Food should be stored in properly labeled containers on clean racks, shelves, dollies or other clean surface in such a manner, and such a height, as to be protected from contamination.

E. Display and Service

1. Glass guards should be used to protect unwrapped food from contamination from customers.
2. Suitable utensils should be used to reduce manual contact with food.
3. Condiments should be provided in dispensers that protect against contamination.
4. Food that has been subjected to possible contamination by the customer cannot be saved or reused.

F. Cleanliness of Equipment and Utensils

1. After each use, all tableware, dishes, glasses, and trays should be thoroughly cleaned and sanitized.

2. All kitchen equipment and surfaces should be thoroughly cleaned and sanitized.
3. The cooking surfaces of grills and griddles should be cleaned at least once each day they are used, and should be free of encrusted grease deposits and other soil.
4. Surfaces not used for food preparation—fans, counters, shelves etc.—should be cleaned as necessary to keep them free of dust, dirt, food particles, grease, and other debris.
5. Detergents are to be rinsed off food-contact surfaces.
6. After utensils are cleaned, they should be handled in such a way to avoid touching the part which will come in contact with food.
7. Adequate storage should be provided for clean equipment.
8. Cleaned equipment and utensils should be air-dried before being stored.

Know Your Way Around

It is important for principals to know their way around the cafeteria. This operation is an important one for any school. It can be a source of school pride, or it can be a problem for the principal. How well the principal addresses the points in this chapter may make the difference.

The principal is expected to set the tone in the building. This includes meeting with the cafeteria manager to review and emphasize the proper philosophy. The material in this chapter is a good place to start and can be used to develop a handbook for your food service staff.

Points to remember:

- Do not allow stealing, either in the form of taking leftovers or eating breakfasts or lunches without paying. It soon adds up to a share of what could and should be profits.
- Sanitation, good hygiene, and proper work habits are imperative. Lack of either can result in epidemic sickness or in workman's compensation claims.

JOB DESCRIPTION—MANAGER/COOK

Responsible to: the building principal.

General duties: to supervise, direct and participate in the preparation and serving of student lunches.

Specific duties:

(1) Prepares menus to be served in the building and assures distribution to students and staff in advance
(2) Assists other cooks in food preparation and serving
(3) Requisitions all food supplies
(4) Determines portions and quality control of food served
(5) Maintains required inventory records
(6) Checks invoices and prepares monthly report or purchases
(7) Evaluates the job performance of assigned cafeteria personnel
(8) Recommends the dismissal or reprimanding of unsatisfactory subordinates
(9) Verifies deliveries and invoices, and verifies invoices for payment by the school district
(10) Maintains a neat and clean kitchen, and adheres to sanitary regulations
(11) Counts all cafeteria receipts daily, and makes out bank deposit slips
(12) Establishes good rapport with students, teaching staff, school administrators, civic groups, and the general public
(13) Performs other related duties as assigned

JOB DESCRIPTION—COOK

Responsible to: the cafeteria manager.
General duties: to prepare and serve student lunches
Specific duties:

(1) Follows the directions of the cafeteria manager
(2) Adheres strictly to prescribed recipes
(3) Works diligently at the specific task assigned, and offers help to others when needed
(4) Acquaints herself/himself with every procedure in the lunchroom
(5) Maintains an orderly and clean work area
(6) Prepares and serves food in an attractive manner
(7) Adheres rigidly to sanitary practices
(8) Maintains a clean and neat personal appearance

(9) Establishes a good rapport with students, teaching staff, school administrators, civic groups, and the general public
(10) Performs other related duties as assigned

SUMMARY

This chapter presented lists of standards for the principal to check when examining the food service area in the school. Emphasis was placed on safety and sanitation and the issue of leftover food. The following chapter discusses the issue of student discipline and how it can be managed in the school.

THE PRINCIPAL'S CASEBOOK

The Case of the Missing Meatloaf

Mrs. Bracken has been the head of the cafeteria for five years and has worked in food services throughout the district for nearly twenty years. She knows her job. Her paperwork is always on time. Although the cafeteria did not make a profit, it was not too deeply in the red either.

Dr. Eaton has been principal in this building for only two years. He has been pleased with the job his cafeteria personnel have done, and was surprised when the assistant superintendent for business called him to tell him to start watching the cafeteria staff and Mrs. Bracken very closely.

After several minutes of discussion, the assistant superintendent told Dr. Eaton that several of the neighbors and a couple of PTA mothers had called the superintendent to complain that their children were not being served enough at lunch, but that the cafeteria ladies were taking home packages of leftovers every day.

Questions to Consider

- Should Dr. Eaton confront Mrs. Bracken with the allegation?
- How much attention should the principal pay to the neighbors and PTA mothers?
- How much attention should Dr. Eaton pay to the assistant superintendent?

- Should the cafeteria workers be allowed to take home leftovers without proper payment? Should free leftovers be a perk of the school district?
- If caught in this act, what, if anything, should be done about these ladies?

REFERENCES

The lists of items in this chapter have been adapted from the following three sources: *Guidelines and Regulations from the United States Department of Agriculture*, *Twinsburg City School Food Service Manual*, and the *Kokomo High School Food Service Manual.*

CHAPTER 8

Student Discipline

INTRODUCTION

No matter what the size of the school is or what grade levels are included, it is imperative that the principal assume direct responsibility for the atmosphere in the school. All students must be provided with a clean, safe school that has a controlled learning environment. Students have the right to come to school to learn. They should not fear that they will be attacked or harmed in any way, nor will their learning be hampered in any way.

In order for this to be a reality, the principal needs to be certain that order and discipline prevail. While the subject of this chapter is student discipline, the intent is not to suggest a heavy-handed, prison-like atmosphere. Rather, this chapter will discuss a positive approach to discipline wherever that is possible, and discuss the legal implications for student discipline when punitive action must be taken.

A POSITIVE ATMOSPHERE

When the word *discipline* is mentioned, most people think of something negative: punishment, paddling, hitting, sitting in the corner. On the other hand, when it is said that someone is *self-disciplined,* this concept is considered very positive. Discipline should not always be considered negative. The best form of discipline is that which encourages self-discipline or self-control. It is the principal's responsibility to set the tone for discipline in his/her school, and to encourage policies which foster self-discipline.

English and Black (1986), in their book on school administration, point out the following:

> . . . If the principal is a warden, you've got a prison. If the principal is a

> despot, you have a police state. If the principal is a wimp, you have chaos. The principal doesn't "buddy up" with the kids, use slang that is in vogue, tell off-color jokes, or horse play with the kids. A leader of kids doesn't act like a kid. . . . The principal is an adult. The principal is someone who cares and deeply believes in the potential for kids to become competent, caring human beings. . . . It colors every action he or she takes. (p. 97)

Curwin and Mendler (1980) suggest a school-wide discipline concept, involving a team approach. Principals should consider a team approach and what it can do for the school. This concept can develop and nurture an atmosphere of mutual respect and trust in the school. This approach not only involves the students and teachers, but also the classified staff as well.

THE TEAM APPROACH TO DISCIPLINE

The Principal

The principal sets the tone and establishes the climate in the building. Everything else becomes a reflection of the principal's attitude. The principal sets the pace and leads the team.

The Assistant Principal

The assistant substitutes for the principal whenever the need arises. The principal and the assistant must agree on their philosophy of discipline and how it will be handled. Typically, the assistant principal has the major responsibility for student discipline in the school. Two things are important to remember: (1) the principal must still play a leadership role in establishing the climate in the school, even though an assistant may carry out day-to-day disciplinary actions. (2) The principal must be sure that the assistant carries out his/her disciplinary duties according to the principal's philosophy.

The Guidance Counselor

Some guidance personnel would object to even being mentioned as part of a disciplinary team. They feel that counselors should have nothing to do with discipline. Yet, counseling should be a part of the disciplinary process. This does not mean that counselors have to assign disciplinary measures to students. It could mean that counselors can offer a place where students can cool off and discuss their situations. Counselors can gently guide and mold a student into seeing what is right and what is wrong. They can be patient and understanding, building trust with the student. At the same time, the counselor has to be a part of the team and reinforce the school's disciplinary policy.

The Classroom Teacher

Teachers may be the most important members of the disciplinary team. Teachers generally know the students better than do the other team members. Because of the nature of the teaching-learning process, teachers are responsible for setting parameters, having formal expectations, and insisting that the students behave in a certain manner in class. As a result, the teacher is important in the discipline of students throughout the school, both in academic pursuits and in extracurricular activities.

The Custodial Staff

It is imperative that a clean and safe learning environment be maintained. The principal must teach the custodians that they are not just cleaning a building but are making an environment more conductive to learning. Continual cleaning, proper maintenance, painting, and the removal of graffiti will help produce this environment. Chapter 3 discussed the necessity of the principal and custodian working together for the safety and cleanliness of the building, and stressed the importance of conducting a regular building walk-through together.

Principals must convince the custodial staff that clean and well-maintained classrooms, restrooms, and public areas contribute to the psychological well-being of the students (and the staff, as well). When a custodian can give students a wholesome environment, a smile, and a warm "Hello," it affects the whole school. It works both ways—good student discipline makes the custodian's job easier, and good building maintenance and cleaning helps with student discipline.

The Cafeteria Staff

Lunch time should be a time of friendly camaraderie for students, not a time when they have to eat in silence, or a time when they are allowed to shout across the room. The cafeteria staff, monitors, teachers, and principal must work together to train students how to behave in the cafeteria. A friendly face on the cafeteria serving line, a positive attitude by the staff, and a good meal will all contribute to better conduct in the cafeteria. Lunch should be a pleasant experience, and the food service staff can help start this experience off in a positive way.

The School Secretary

How is the secretary part of the team? The office secretary is really on the front lines, along with the teachers. She is usually the first person students see when they are sent to the office from a classroom after a problem, or from the cafeteria after getting too loud, or from the gym after a fight, or from the hallways after running. Throughout the day, the secretary is confronted by students who have been sent to the office for disciplinary reasons – students who are usually upset at someone or some situation. It is tough for the secretary to be the one person who stands at the counter and receives these students. The secretary must learn how to handle these situations. She can either calm the student down or make things worse, depending on how she handles the students. A calm voice and a little kindness will go far to help quiet down the student. While the secretary cannot minimize what the students have done, she can try to calm them down, have them wait quietly for the administrator, and try to reassure them that they will be treated fairly.

The School Bus Driver

A lot of time is spent training bus drivers to drive, know safety rules, handle emergencies, and know the equipment. These things are very important. Drivers should also be trained to deal with students. Discipline problems do occur on buses, and these problems often overflow into the school. Principals have to work with bus drivers on how to handle students on the bus, and when to refer problems to the office after the bus arrives at school. Drivers need to be mature, stable adults who enjoy being around children, but who believe in having them behave properly.

While the hiring process is sometimes elaborate for replacing teachers, it is usually relatively simple for hiring classified staff. However, that does not mean proper attention should not be paid to this process. With respect to bus drivers, principals should work with the superintendent or transportation director to find drivers who are competent both in the driving phase and in handling children. Finally, principals may want to use *Assertive Discipline for Bus Drivers* (1987), written by Lee and Marlene Canter.

The Student Council

Stradley and Aspinall (1975) feel that student councils are important to the atmosphere in the schools: "When problems occur, the student council can help solve the conflicts. Student council faculty advisors should counsel the membership on what the democratic process means and why its strengths lie in unity and purpose" (p. 89).

Principals should never underestimate the power of using the student council as a collective member of the discipline team. Guided by a competent faculty advisor, the student council should not be in opposition to the administration. The administration needs to show the council that it wants to see discipline handled in such a way that students can be encouraged to have self-control.

It is suggested that the principal empower the student council to organize a grievance committee to hear problems and complaints from the students. This should help with the credibility of the council, and will offer a forum for recalcitrant students to air their problems and concerns with fellow students.

If structured properly, this team approach to discipline can help solve many of the minor problems that can take up so much of the teacher's or principal's time. With everyone working together to maintain the same attitude and philosophy toward discipline, the expectations and the outcomes should be the same. As a result, the principal, staff, and students will have a much smoother running school.

DYSFUNCTIONAL AND ANTISOCIAL BEHAVIOR

No matter how well the team approach to discipline works, there will always be a few students who will not assume responsibility for their own behavior. As a result, procedures must be developed to handle these students. While there is the temptation to just throw these students out of school ("and let his parents deal with him!"), this action is at cross-purposes to what we are trying to accomplish in school–to produce good citizens who can think, judge, and make good decisions about their actions. Thus, the school should make an effort to counsel these students into proper behavior.

Of course, the school cannot do this alone. Parents must work with the schools to try to correct inappropriate behavior, which is sometimes easier said than done, when parents cannot or will not join the school team in trying to help their children.

In spite of all this effort, there are times when students must be removed from school. When their behavior threatens others or disrupts the school sufficiently, students have to be suspended or expelled.

However, in removing students from school, two things have to be kept in mind—special education situations and due process.

Disruptive Special Education Students

Since 1975, federal law has mandated that no student can be excluded from school because of a handicapping condition. If the school or a private sector psychologist has stated that a student has a problem, and has been identified as seriously emotionally disturbed or severely behaviorally handicapped, that student cannot be removed from school if the offense committed is related to the handicapping condition.

Schools must establish procedures for holding a formal special education procedure to determine if an offense is related to the student's handicapping condition. If it is, further procedures must be developed for dealing with the student and the behavior without removing the student from school. Since the Education for All Handicapped Children Act was passed in 1975, schools should already have such procedures in place. Of course, if the behavior is not related to the handicapping condition, the student may be removed from school in accordance with the procedures developed for other students, unless state law prohibits it. Franklin and Braun (1992) write that in Illinois, "the law is unsettled as to whether a special education student may be expelled from school when the behavior giving rise to the discipline is not related to the child's handicapping condition" (p. 209).

Due Process Rights for Students

The Fifth Amendment of the Constitution states (in part) that no person shall ". . . be deprived of life, liberty, or property, without due process of law. . . ." Seventy-seven years later, Congress passed the Fourteenth Amendment, extending these rights to the state level: ". . . nor shall any State deprive any person of life, liberty, or property, without due process of law; nor deny to any person within its jurisdiction the equal protection of the laws."

Although this latter Amendment was passed in 1868, it was interpreted to apply only to adults. As stated in Chapter 6, *In re Gault* (1967) resulted in a ruling which stated that children, as well as adults, are entitled to due process. Thus, it is a relatively recent concept to give due process (by law) to students in school. One of the first cases dealing with this concept was taken to the United States Supreme Court in 1975.

Goss v. *Lopez*

In this case, Lopez, a student in a Columbus, Ohio, school was suspended from school (with others) for a disturbance in the cafeteria. He had not been given any due process prior to or after his suspension. He had just been told to go home. The Supreme Court ruled that the student was entitled to a hearing, and also that the Ohio statute that was used to suspend the student was unconstitutional. The Court said that suspensions can damage the student's standings with teachers and other students, and interfere with education and employment. An informal hearing should be held within minutes after the incident, with the administration telling the student about his misconduct. The Court also recognized that there are times when immediate removal is necessary with the hearing being held later. The Court did *not* require that the student could secure counsel, cross-examine witnesses, or call witnesses. This case dealt with a short suspension (ten days or less), not an expulsion. More formal procedures are probably necessary for a longer suspension or expulsion.

As a result of *Goss* v. *Lopez* and similar decisions, administrators had to establish procedures for dealing with the due process rights of students. Many school districts put these procedures in writing and developed forms to help the administrator follow the district procedures. In a similar vein, administrators put the school rules in writing, published them in student handbooks, and distributed them to the students, sometimes requiring the students to sign a form that they received the handbooks.

Kinds of Due Process

The due process under discussion thus far is called *procedural* due process. In brief, it requires the administrator to tell the student what the violation was, to give the student an opportunity to give his/her side of the incident, and to allow the student a fair and impartial hearing. As stated earlier, the formality of the procedures and hearing increases with the increase in the penalty that could be levied.

Another due process is *substantive* due process. As Kimbrough and Burkett (1990) say, "Substantive due process is less precise than procedural due process. It is highly discretionary but embraces the spirit of the need for fair treatment of all people, including students" (p. 218). This means that schools need to establish rules which are fair, clearly stated, and reasonable. Also, the punishment which is given for the violation of a rule should be in proportion to the violation. Finally, the rules should be applied in a fair manner. Some students should not be singled out for punishment while others go free, nor should one group (minority or female, for example) receive different treatment than another group.

CORPORAL PUNISHMENT

Corporal punishment has always been controversial, but the debate has increased since the due process and student rights decisions of the 1960s and 1970s. The Supreme Court in *Ingraham* v. *Wright,* ruled that corporal punishment was not an example of cruel and unusual punishment (which is outlawed by the Eighth Amendment to the Constitution). Thus, it is up to individual states, districts, or administrators to decide whether to use corporal punishment. An administrator should know whether the state has any restrictions (or procedural requirements), or whether the local school board has established any prohibitions. If the state legislature or the local board of education has prohibited corporal punishment, the principal's feelings about its use are moot. On the other hand, if both allow this punishment to be used, the principal should do the following:

- Check with the superintendent to get his/her views on its use.
- Check to see what has been done in the past in this particular school – is this punishment common or rare in the school?

- Depending on the principal's philosophy on corporal punishment, discuss the issue with the faculty, assistants, and counselors.
- Find out whether state law or local policy allows parents to submit a request that corporal punishment not be administered to their children.
- If permitted, and if the decision is to use corporal punishment, the principal should give the student due process prior to the punishment—inform the child of the misbehavior and give him/her an opportunity to discuss it. Other procedures may be required by the state or by the board.
- A second staff member should be present during the punishment and, if possible, during the due process given prior to the hearing.
- Parents should be notified of the punishment and the reasons for it.
- Like all school punishment, corporal punishment must be administered in a reasonable manner, in good faith, and without malice.

ASSERTIVE DISCIPLINE

One of the programs which has been found effective by some teachers is Lee Canter's (1980) program of assertive discipline. While there may be teachers who are not able to use this method effectively, or those who have found a different but an equally effective way to establish discipline, it is worthwhile to show one adaption of the Canter program. This is shown in Figure 8.1.

Detention and Inside Suspension

One of the normal punishments used by teachers is detention. This can take place after school or before school and, in some schools, on Saturday. For many students, the worst thing that can happen is to lose their freedom, to be restricted to the school when everyone else is at home or at play. Detention is an alternative to suspension. In fact, some administrators give students a choice—take a suspension or take a detention. Many will choose the suspension. Detention not only allows students to go to classes instead of being suspended, it forces them to

Teachers are told that they have certain rights regarding discipline:

1. They can establish a classroom structure and routine that provides the optimal learning environment in light of their own strengths and weaknesses.
2. They have the right to determine and request appropriate behavior from the students.
3. They have the right to ask for help from parents and the administration when they need assistance with a student.

Teachers should develop a good set of rules for the classroom. Here are some guidelines for the rules:

1. They should be short and to the point.
2. There should not be too many—about five.
3. They should express the teacher's needs.
4. They should cover as much as possible that can happen.
5. They should be stated in behavioral terms.
6. If the rule does not work, change it.

Below are some examples of possible classroom rules:

1. Be in your seat ready to work with appropriate materials on time.
2. There is no talking without permission.
3. Follow directions the first time I give them.
4. No one can eat, chew, or drink in the classroom without permission.
5. Stay in your seat unless you have permission to get up.

Here are some general guidelines:

1. The teacher must be comfortable with the punishment for a student who does not obey a rule.
2. The consequence for the student must be unpleasant.
3. An early or late detention is usually a part of the punishment system, increasing with each occurrence.
4. The teacher must recognize the difference between minor and major discipline problems and have appropriate punishments.
5. Every student must be treated alike.
6. Every day is a new day with a clean slate for each student.
7. If a certain punishment does not work, change it.
8. Inform and involve parents and administrators.

***Figure 8.1** A Modification of the Program Used at Kokomo, Indiana Schools, Based on the Work of Lee Canter.*

spend extra time at school, which can be productive if the school uses the detention time for academic study. Of course, there are times when students have to be removed from school to protect others or school property.

Another alternative to suspending a student outside of school is inside (or in-school) suspension. In this punishment, students are suspended from all classes and activities and are restricted to one area for a certain period of time. The advantage is that the student does not get the freedom to leave school. Also, for younger students whose parents are not at home, it allows the administration to suspend them without sending them to a vacant house or wondering whether they will even go home. Some administrators may even suspend a student inside the school but, for one reason or another, permit them to attend one or two classes. Principals should remember that this is still a suspension, and they should follow the usual due process procedures.

For those principals who may want some guidelines for detention and inside suspension, Appendix B is included at the end of the book. It also contains a sample letter to parents, and a teacher assignment sheet for detention.

SUMMARY

This chapter presented a view of the team approach to school discipline, a discussion of discipline of special education students, corporal punishment, due process procedures for students, assertive discipline, and detention or inside suspension. The next chapter deals with the role of the principal in pupil transportation.

THE PRINCIPAL'S CASEBOOK

The Case of the Cafeteria Crasher

John Miller, a relatively new student in your high school, ran into the student cafeteria, starting yelling at another student who was eating, and then grabbed him around the neck, throwing him and his chair on the floor. The cafeteria supervisor witnessed the entire matter and got there before any fists were thrown. He brought Miller into the office to see you, the assistant principal. As the student went into your office, the secretary said, "I think John may be special education, but I'm not sure." One of the counselors, getting her mail, said, "I don't think so, but you'd better check."

Questions to Consider

- What would you, as the assistant principal, say to Miller when you two enter your office?
- How would you check to see if he is a special education student?
- What does "special education student" mean?
- How would you proceed if he is a special education student? Is there more than one way? What if he is not special education?
- What punishment is appropriate?
- What procedures would you follow in giving out this punishment?

REFERENCES

Canter, L. and M. Canter. 1987. *Assertive Discipline for Bus Drivers.* Los Angeles: Lee Canter and Assoc.

Canter, L. and M. Canter. 1980. *Assertive Discipline: A Take Charge Approach for Today's Educator.* Los Angeles: Lee Canter and Assoc.

Curwin, R. L. and A. N. Mendler. 1980 *The Discipline Book: A Complete Guide to School and Classroom Management.* Reston, VA: Reston Publ. Co., Inc.

English, F. and J. Black. 1986. *What They Don't Tell You in Schools of Education about School Administration.* Lancaster PA: Technomic Publishing Co., Inc.

Franklin, D. L. and B. A. Braun. 1992. *Illinois School Law Survey.* Springfield, IL: Illinois Association of School Boards.

Goss v. *Lopez,* 95 S. Ct. 729, 419 U.S. 565, 42 L. Ed. 2d 725 (1975).

Ingraham v. *Wright,* 97 S. Ct. 1401, 430 U.S. 651 51 L. Ed. 2d 711 (1977).

In re Gault, 387 U.S. 1, Ariz., (1967).

Kimbrough, R. B. and C. W. Burkett. 1990. *The Principalship: Concepts and Practices.* Englewood Cliffs, N.J.: Prentice-Hall.

Stradley, W. E. and R. D. Aspinall. 1975. *Discipline in the Junior High/Middle School: A Handbook for Teachers, Counselors, and Administrators.* New York: The Center for Applied Research in Education.

United States Constitution.

CHAPTER 9

The Principal and Pupil Transportation

INTRODUCTION

Every principal is involved with pupil transportation, whether through the busing of children to and from school, through field trips, or for the transportation of athletic teams and fans. This chapter will discuss procedures for dealing with daily transportation, and will suggest safety guidelines for bus drivers.

PROCEDURES FOR DAILY TRANSPORTATION

Although principals at all grade levels are involved with the daily transportation of students (unless the district is one in which the students walk to school or are transported by independent carriers), the elementary principal must plan procedures more carefully than principals at other grade levels, simply because of the age of the pupils.

Young elementary students cannot read and may not know their home addresses. Thus, the elementary principal must establish ways to move several sections of lower-grade students onto the correct buses each afternoon. Prior to the first day of school, the principal should know the buses which will come to the school, the bus numbers, and the names of the drivers. Each driver should work with the principal to prepare a list of the children who will ride on each bus. To help students identify the correct bus, it may be helpful to color code the buses or put some familiar figures, like Mickey Mouse, on the various buses which go to the school. Planning like this will help reduce the number of bus problems which occur the first few days.

Both elementary school and middle school/junior high school principals should meet their buses each morning and each afternoon. This practice has several benefits—it reduces bus problems, it sets a good tone for the rest of the day, it enables the principal to get to know some students, it reduces horseplay immediately before and after school, and it is a practice the bus drivers will appreciate. They will tend to see the principal as someone who is working with them on transportation rather than someone who is in the building, not concerned with the problems they encounter in their jobs.

Middle school and high school principals also have to be concerned with athletic transportation, fan, and band buses. Depending on the size of the school, an athletic director or a school secretary may be able to register students for fan buses, and arrange for buses for athletic teams. Often, the school has faculty who supervise the fan buses, and coaches and band directors who take charge of the buses carrying their members. Likewise, field trips are usually arranged by the sponsoring faculty member through the school office.

Regardless of the use of buses—for daily transportation or for special events—the principal must remember that from a legal standpoint the school day (and the school's responsibility) is extended by these bus trips. The school's responsibility begins at the bus stop in the morning and extends to the drop off point in the afternoon, or to the return of the trip from the special event at night. The principal is responsible for everything that happens during school, and this includes pupil transportation.

THE BUS DRIVER-PRINCIPAL TEAM

The principal should make an effort to work with the drivers and establish a driver-principal team. This team should discuss where and when buses unload in the morning and load in the afternoon. The team should also discuss bus rules and loading procedures, and know the discipline procedures that will be used for violation of the rules by students. Figure 9.1 is an example of a memorandum which might be sent from a principal to the bus drivers stating the results of a discussion between the principal and drivers. (Also note the poor example, as well.)

BUS SAFETY

The prime concern of the transportation program must be safety. The principal needs to examine the bus routes into the school area, the lanes

To: Bus Drivers for Middle and Elementary School
From: Jeff Aper, Principal
Re: Bus Procedures
Morning Unloading Time:
7:45–7:50 AM Middle School; tardy bell rings at 7:55
8:10–8:15 AM Elementary School; tardy bell rings at 8:20

Students are not to be unloaded before the above listed times. If you arrive early, sit with your students until the school opens. Try to adjust your arrival time for future trips.

Afternoon Loading Time:
2:50 PM Elementary School
3:10 PM Middle School

Buses are not to leave before these times.

Discipline Procedures

1. For the first violation, give the student a warning and make a notation of it.
2. For the next violation, write up a discipline report and give it to me.
3. For any further violations, write up a report for me. In general, I will meet with the student on the first write-up and issue a warning. Later violations will result in parent conferences and suspensions from school or suspensions from bus service.
4. While you may be tempted to remove a rider from the bus, bring the student to school. You can then write up the misbehavior for me to review or have the student remain on the bus until all other riders leave and then escort the student to the office.
5. Rules and regulations should be discussed with your riders on the first day. You should be firm, but fair and consistent. Treat all students alike.
6. If a student is not at his/her stop at the appropriate time, you should warn the student and make a note of the tardiness. If this happens again, notify the office. (Be sure to be on time yourself, weather permitting.)

Thank you for your continuing help in beginning and ending the day at our school. Remember that I am available to help with any bus problem that you have. Unless there is an emergency or I am away from school, I will meet the buses each morning and afternoon. Together we should be able to stop potential problems before they become serious. By doing this, we can make both our jobs more enjoyable.

A Poor Example

Below is an example of a poorly written memorandum to bus drivers. It is included here because, unfortunately, it was actually used in a school district. All the errors are still here.

I had a meeting with five bus drivers with concerns involving myself drivers and mechanics, this is the results of that meeting.

When weather and time permits the mechanics will wash buses however there are times when weather permits and time does not remember repairs must come first.

This is also the case of washing windows when a bus comes in for service windows will be washed if time permits. (Front & Rear Only)

***Figure 9.1** Memo from Principal to Bus Drivers.*

There is a sign up sheet for use of all sub buses please be sure you check oil, water, fuel and clean inside when you return it fuel should be added if it's below 1/2 tank. (Be sure you sign the bus out and in.

Please be sure your bus is within 100 miles of service when you schedule it and don't forget to drop it off. [School name] Elem has a parking problem in the PM so bus #24 will try parking on the East side to see if this helps please cooperate any way you can to help out.

The JVS buses will try letting the JVS students off at the front door at the high school in the PM this may save some confusion in the parking lot in the evening.

Please leave room for drivers to get the sub buses out of parking in the AM–PM.

Please turn your gas cards in the first day of the month make sure your bus number and ending mileage is marked. Also try and fill out absent slips each week I take them up each Monday.

Please use the strobe lights only when we have inclement weather other wise they will not catch attention of other drivers when necessary.

Strobe lights are being put on all buses please be patient you might want to ask the mechanic if he has time that you would like one we are trying to get a few each month to spread the cost out.

Please stay with your bus when you fuel you can not sweep your bus while fueling we have had some spills do to this so please stay right at the fill.

Please when calling in on the CB state your bus number and your problem and if you need another bus we can sometimes hear you and can't get back to you but the mechanic can get on the road while I try and get back to you. (Also your location).

If you need a window scraper ask the mechanic if we don't have any in stock we will get them.

Figure 9.1 (continued) *Memo from Principal to Bus Drivers.*

where the buses park at the school, and the area for loading and unloading at the school site. Markings and/or signs must be available so that other drivers, as well as those who walk to school, know where buses enter the school property, park, load/unload, and exit the property. Students who ride the buses should be able to enter and exit buses near a curb or sidewalk, away from all other traffic.

State and national guidelines (like the Highway Safety Program Standard 17) require schools to hold driver safety programs and student evacuation drills. The principal should work with the drivers to see that these are held and that students behave properly, just as the principal sees that fire drills or tornado drills are properly scheduled and carried out. Evacuation procedures and safe riding practices are listed in Figure 9.2.

The principal should discuss rules, regulations, and expectations with the drivers before school begins. Often, there is a one-day driver orientation prior to the start of school where these activities can occur. The comments made in Figure 9.1 can be a basis for such a discussion. In addition, Figure 9.3 lists many rules, suggestions, and tips for bus drivers. The principal can sift through them to find those which are

Evacuation Procedures

The objective of the drill is prompt, orderly evacuation. Speed alone is not the objective.

1. Students should exit from the door that is closest, either the front or rear door.
2. The pattern for leaving is to alternate entering the aisle seat by seat, with the students on the door side entering the aisle first, followed by the students on the driver side.
3. The first student who exits from the rear emergency door should hold the door open and extend a hand to help the next student. The second student, upon exiting, should help the rest of the students down from the bus. Ideally, the third student leaving this exit should lead the students away from the bus to a safe area.
4. The first student leaving the front door should lead those riders to a safe area away from the bus.
5. The driver should remain on the bus until all students have left the bus. There should be a clear command like "Evacuate the bus!" from the driver. (When timing the drills, the time starts at this command and ends when the driver has exited the bus.)

Safe Riding Practices

1. Students should be seated at all times, not in the aisles. The driver should notify the principal if a bus is overloaded.
2. While reasonable conversation is permitted, loud or boisterous activity is not allowed.
3. The driver needs to maintain control of all doors and windows. Students should not be allowed to open doors or windows until instructed to do so by the driver. The driver must insist, in the safety orientation for students, that the emergency door is just that, for emergencies, and cannot be used for exiting unless the driver allows it to be opened. (Sometimes it is used for loading/unloading special equipment, like band instruments, under supervision and with permission. Obviously, this is not a normal routine.) Students must understand that they cannot throw anything in the bus or from the bus. When windows are permitted to be opened to the proper level, students cannot extend arms or heads out these windows. Similarly, although it may not involve safety as much as the above comments, students should not be allowed to yell out the windows any more than they are allowed to yell within the bus.
4. Obviously, smoking is not permitted on a school bus, but the driver should also warn that striking matches and lighting lighters are prohibited. The danger of fire on a bus, with all the books, papers, and clothing on board, should be stressed. Drivers are not to smoke on the bus or school property.
5. Students must be taught to remain seated until the bus has come to a full stop. Airline passengers have learned to do this, and school bus passengers should learn too.

Some of the above comments were taken from Transportation Manuals of Twinsburg City School, Twinsburg, Ohio, and Kokomo High School, Indiana, and are based on U.S. Department of Transportation standards.

***Figure 9.2** Evacuation Procedures/Safe Riding Practices.*

1. Make only one drop off at each school.
2. Do not pass other buses on school grounds.
3. Drivers must stop at stop signs, including those at the school.
4. Do not back up on school grounds. (The principal should arrange lanes so buses can always pull forward from their parking places.)
5. If you leave the bus, take the key with you.
6. Drivers should use their seat belts. (Whether students use belts depends on state and local laws and procedures.)
7. If you wear corrective glasses, wear a strap around your neck connected to the glasses.
8. On field trips and athletic trips, stop only where authorized. If all students are to be brought back to the school, do not let them off along the way.
9. Do not alter bus routes (except for emergency or weather reasons). Do not assume that a student will not be at a stop. Stop at all scheduled stops.
10. Always do a pretrip check—gasoline and other gauges, lights, tires, etc.
11. Do not open the door at a stop until the bus has made a complete stop.
12. Instruct students where to stand when waiting for a bus, and where and how to cross the street when exiting the bus. Students should cross in front of the bus at a distance of about ten feet.
13. Drivers should not use earphones, loud radios, Walkmans, etc.
14. Be friendly, but not too familiar.
15. Learn the students' names as well and as soon as you can.
16. You can improve discipline if your riders call you Mr., Mrs., Miss, instead of by your first name.
17. When there is trouble, try to find the person responsible. Do not punish the whole bus.
18. Do not threaten to report someone and fail to do it.
19. Since the disciplinary actions you can use are limited, do not threaten to do something which you cannot do.
20. Watch your language. Students should not be allowed to use inappropriate language and you should not do so either.

Some of the above are revisions of rules listed in the Transportation Manuals of Twinsburg City Schools, Ohio, and Kokomo High School, Indiana, and are based on U. S. Department of Transportation standards.

Figure 9.3 *A List of Rules/Suggestions/Tips for Bus Drivers.*

useful for an orientation day, or those which can be used to prepare a written list for the drivers.

Principals should impress upon bus drivers the serious responsibility they have. The lives of children are entrusted to them. Safety on the road must be the prime concern. At the same time, the driver teaches students proper behavior, maintains discipline, instructs students on safety procedures, teaches students to associate and cooperate with others, and sets the tone for the beginning of every school day. For some parents, the school bus is the only visible sign of the school, and the bus driver is the only school employee seen on a regular basis. A smile and a friendly wave to parents who are visible helps with the school's relationship with the community.

Bus drivers do more than just drive buses. They help shape attitudes toward driving itself, and toward safety and fair play. They provide a necessary service, serve as a link to the community, and represent the school.

SUMMARY

This chapter discussed the role of the bus driver in the school program, and gave suggestions for the principal to use in the areas of procedures, bus discipline, safe riding practices, and rules and suggestions. The next chapter addresses the building of the school schedule.

THE PRINCIPAL'S CASEBOOK

The Case of the Sweltering Students

It is late spring and you have just returned home from a track meet. The telephone rings, and Mrs. Able, the parent of a fifth-grade student, is calling to complain that her son and six others were unfairly punished by their bus driver, Mrs. Armstrong.

According to Mrs. Able, the day was hot and the boys put down their windows as far as they could go to get some relief from the heat. Mrs. Armstrong told the boys that they did not have her permission to lower the windows at all, let alone that far. As a result, she told them to put their windows up for the ride home. Now, Mrs. Able says, the boys are sick and vomiting, and her husband wants to sue the driver and the school and speak at the next school board meeting. Mrs. Able says, "What are you going to do about it?"

Questions to Consider

- As principal, what plan of action would you take following your conversation with Mrs. Able?
- Who will you contact? In what order?
- Is Mrs. Armstrong's punishment (if reported accurately) appropriate? Should she have done something else?
- What will you tell Mrs. Armstrong? Mr. and Mrs. Able?

ACKNOWLEDGEMENT

Our thanks to Susan Webster, experienced bus driver, for her reading of this chapter and her opinions on the content.

REFERENCE

National Highway Traffic Safety Administration, *Highway Safety Program Standard 17, Pupil Transportation Safety.* Washington, D.C.: United States Department of Transportation.

CHAPTER 10

*The Principal as Master Schedule Maker**

INTRODUCTION

The process of scheduling has changed over the years in some districts. Principals who years ago would have used a set of cards with holes around the edges now depend on computers to combine student course selections with parameters from the administration to develop the schedule. (See Appendix C for information on management software.)

There are still many principals, especially in smaller districts, who must schedule students manually. New principals who have an assistant or counselor with experience in scheduling are fortunate. Many new principals find that they have to build a schedule with little or no help and no experience. This chapter is included in those principals.

The first section will discuss the high school schedule. This will be followed by sections on scheduling the middle school and the elementary school.

SCHEDULING THE HIGH SCHOOL

The Course Offerings

What courses should be available to students? That depends on the community, the state requirements, accrediting agency standards, the

*Gene Parks, former associate principal at Kokomo, Indiana, now retired, contributed the initial material for the section on high school scheduling, with the help of Fran McKee.

Dr. Hazel Loucks, assistant professor of educational administration at Southern Illinois University at Carbondale, made suggestions for the high school section, and wrote the sections on scheduling the middle school and the elementary school.

career choices of the graduates, the financial condition of the school district, the space available, the demographics of the student population, and the teaching qualifications of the staff. If most students go immediately into the job market, the curriculum should reflect that fact. If most go to a four-year university, the curriculum should have other courses available. In the vast majority of high schools, the students choose a variety of career paths, requiring a comprehensive high school curriculum.

A new principal who does not know the community well might want to look at the most recent regional accreditation report for the school (assuming it is accredited by such an agency) and see if there were recommendations for curriculum changes. Also, there is usually a section titled "School and Community" where the principal can learn some of the characteristics of these two areas and see if the school offerings meet the needs of students of the community. The school may have conducted follow-up studies of their graduates, and these can be checked to see what graduates have had to say about their high school programs and what careers they have sought. Other sources of information include school counselors, students, teachers, university admissions officers, and local industry and building trades.

Constructing the Master Schedule

Prior to schedule construction, a calendar of activities is developed by the staff and administration, and distributed to the central administration, school administration, all department chairs, and all counselors in September for the school year beginning the following September. The dates of each activity and the room reservations are posted on the calendar to prevent conflicts.

One master schedule builder that the authors consulted stated that the construction of his master schedule actually starts with the construction of two 4′ × 8′ homosote insulation boards attached to the wall of his office. These boards are painted white and marked off to reflect columns for teacher names and periods in the school day. One board is used for the fall semester and one for the spring semester. (These master schedule boards are available for purchase from school supply companies.) Small rectangles of colored paper are stapled to the board to indicate an assignment in each class period for each teacher and for both semesters. Figure 10.1 shows an example.

Course No. Tchr. No. Rm.

Algebra I

Per. No. Sec. No. Max. Enr

Figure 10.1 *Tag for Schedule Board.*

All teacher preparation periods are indicated by red tags, singletons (courses with only a single section) are placed on orange tags, doubletons are indicated on blue tabs, and special assignments are indicated by white tags. The color-coding approach makes it easy for this schedule maker to check on the distribution of the teacher preparation periods, singletons, and doubletons scheduled during the school day of each semester.

Each department chair is asked to submit a tentative department schedule by mid-November for the next school year. This schedule includes a list of each departmental course, how many sections it would probably have, and tentative teacher assignments during each class period of the school day. This is developed with input from the departmental staff, thus involving teachers in the process. Teachers are often asked to list the courses they would like to teach in order of priority to help the department chair prepare this listing.

The various departments formulate their tentative department schedules on the basis of state-required courses, electives, new courses to be offered, courses to be dropped, equipment available, teacher certification and qualifications, and the interests, needs, and abilities of the students.

A brief description of all departmental courses is printed in a curriculum handbook. This handbook, developed by the individual department staffs, includes course descriptions, credits awarded, minimum grade level, and prerequisites for each course. Copies of the handbook are distributed to all teachers in January.

Special convocations are held for each grade level in February. During these sessions, students are given copies of the curriculum handbook, along with a list of those courses required for that grade level, and a list of the state-required courses. Students are asked to talk to teachers, counselors, and their parents and then indicate their preliminary course selections on a form which is provided for them. It is also helpful to schedule a parent information night for the entry level grade.

Students may be scheduled during their regular English classes, social studies classes, or some other class which all students in a grade level take. Students are asked to indicate alternative courses in priority order in case their original choice cannot be granted. These selections are sent to the counselors for their use when they meet with the students in individual counseling sessions following the convocations. At these sessions, the counselor completes a student election sheet for each student. These sheets are then used to determine how many students in each grade level have selected each course. (Some schools would feed these student election sheets into a computer.) From this point on, the principal should work with the counselors and teachers to develop the master schedule.

The Conflict Matrix

Since the total number of students registered for each class is now known, the principal and the staff advisory group (counselors, teachers, or other persons who can provide expertise) can determine how many classes will be needed in each subject. To see which classes should not be scheduled at the same hour, the principal constructs a *conflict matrix,* or gets one from a computer printout. While this process may not eliminate all conflicts, it should minimize the problem. To give an example, a student will have a scheduling problem if the student wants to take physics II and chorus, and the classes have only one section each, meeting at the same hour. The conflict matrix will prevent many such problems. The conflict matrix plots those one-section classes which, if placed in the same period, would result in conflicts. Figure 10.2 shows an example of a conflict matrix for single-section classes (Jacobson, Reavis and Logsdon, 1963).

Individual preliminary registration cards are checked for each student, and one-section classes are plotted on a tentative schedule. On the conflict matrix shown in Figure 10.2, the tally marks show how many conflicts would appear if those classes were placed on the schedule at the same period. For example, physics II and algebra III would produce

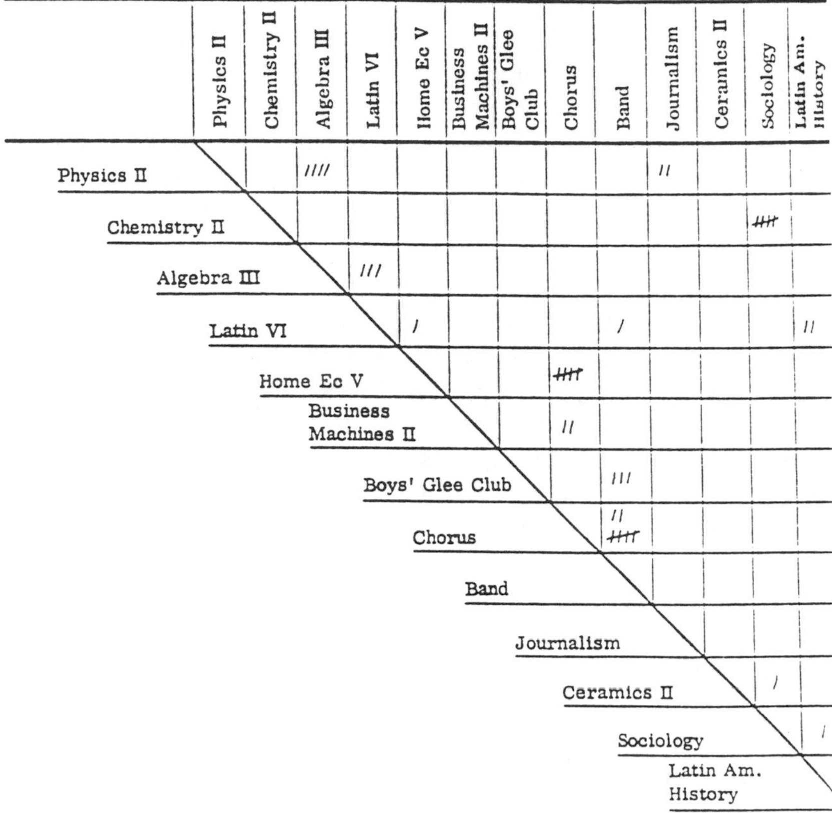

	Physics II	Chemistry II	Algebra III	Latin VI	Home Ec V	Business Machines II	Boys' Glee Club	Chorus	Band	Journalism	Ceramics II	Sociology	Latin Am. History
Physics II			////							//			
Chemistry II												~~////~~	
Algebra III				///									
Latin VI					/				/				//
Home Ec V								~~////~~					
Business Machines II								//					
Boys' Glee Club									///				
Chorus									// ~~////~~				
Band													
Journalism													
Ceramics II												/	
Sociology													/
Latin Am. History													

Figure 10.2 Sample Conflict Matrix.

four student conflicts if scheduled at the same hour; physics II and chorus would not conflict.

The principal, seeing these conflicts, would then change the placement of those one-section classes so as to eliminate the conflicts. A conflict matrix like the one shown can be prepared by hand for a high school of 1,800 students in about seven to nine hours. A computer can be used for the same purpose and do the work quickly. The computer, if available, can also list the students who will have the conflicts. This information can be helpful, so that those students can be located and asked to select different courses that do not conflict. Since most single-section classes are electives (except in small schools), the student may have to select an alternative elective. The principal, in changing the schedule because of conflicts, should remember that the final senior semester should have the fewest conflicts, since this is the last time (before summer school) for seniors to complete work.

After the conflicts have been eliminated or reduced, the principal and the advisory group construct the rest of the master schedule on the large boards, listing course numbers, section numbers, teacher numbers (or names), room numbers, semester numbers, class period numbers, and the maximum capacity for each course section.

In establishing the master schedule, the following should be considered: avoiding conflicts (as discussed), scheduling teacher preparation periods evenly during the day or at special times to allow for common preparation periods for departments, scheduling classes which use the same (limited) equipment in a single classroom at different periods, assigning teacher supervision when needed, and scheduling a course that has two sections so that one section meets in the morning and the other section meets in the afternoon.

After the master schedule is constructed, the students are assigned to classes as they register. Attention should be paid to the size of each section compared to the maximum capacity, and to the number of conflicts which occur. Adjustments may have to be made to the master schedule, such as adding a section, changing a section's placement in the schedule, or scheduling an early-bird or late-bird section (e.g., sections scheduled before or after the normal school day) to avoid conflicts. This, of course, would involve calling the students involved to see if they can come at that time. Again, if a computer is used, these schedule runs can be done more quickly, and conflicts can be resolved more easily.

When the scheduling seems complete, the principal needs to double-check for conflicts, changes in staff, staff assignments, new student requests, room availability, section load against seating, lab positions, negotiated class section maximums, and to see that an adequate number of textbooks is available for each course.

From the master schedule and the assignment of students to the schedule, the principal needs to provide the following, either by hand or computer: teacher class lists, a schedule for each student, room usage lists, and teacher schedules.

Finally, other considerations must be kept in mind as the schedule is constructed: the length of a period, the length of the school day, the number of periods, the transportation schedule for the district, the bell schedule for the school building, the lunchroom schedule and the capacity for each lunch period, and any homeroom or study halls which the school plans to have. It should be mentioned that many schools are reducing or eliminating study halls in their schedules, since these sections are usually merely holding areas for those students who cannot be scheduled into classes during those periods. Also, many schools establish one regular daily schedule and then have one or more alternative schedules for assemblies, early dismissals, late beginnings, and other planned activities.

SCHEDULING THE MIDDLE SCHOOL

If a school district chooses to use a true middle school concept for its students in the middle grades, the scheduling for this school is very different from the scheduling of the high school. The teachers should have a high degree of autonomy in developing the schedule with the principal acting as an advisor. The middle school concept includes team teaching, a block-of-time for some classes, and exploratory periods, all of which require scheduling unique to this school.

Figure 10.3 shows one possible schedule for a middle school consisting of grades six through eight. (Some districts may have other grade ranges due to many different factors, such as facilities, enrollment demands, etc.) Note that, on this particular schedule, band/chorus is scheduled for the first period with no other classes conflicting with it, so that students in all three grades can participate together. Obviously, there are other configurations which would permit larger schools to have different bands for the lower and upper grades, and may even call for more periods of band and chorus.

The advisor/advisee period, scheduled second, is a time for teachers to interact with students on a more personal basis. Topics addressed during this advisor/advisee period may involve problem solving, personal advice conflict management, study skills, group and individual counseling (though the school may have one or more full-time counselors for problems which reach beyond the regular classroom teacher's skills), and student discipline. All professional personnel in the school (and sometimes some staff personnel) are assigned to an advisory period in order to reduce the staff-student ratio. Typically, one staff member is assigned to a small group of twelve to fourteen students. However, two teachers can be assigned to a group of thirty students to allow faculty

P	0	1	2	3	4	5	6	7	8	9
8:15 9:00	8:30 9:00	9:00 9:41	9:41 10:22	10:22 11:03	11:03 11:44	11:44 12:25	12:25 1:06	1:06 1:47	1:47 2:29	2:29 3:11

SIXTH GRADE

P	0	1	2	3	4	5	6	7	8	9
BAND & HONORS CHORUS	T A P	B L O C K			LUNCH & RECESS	B L O C K			EXPL & PE/H	EXPL & PE/H

SEVENTH GRADE

P	0	1	2	3	4	5	6	7	8	9
BAND & HONORS CHORUS	T A P	EXPL & PE/H	EXPL & PE/H	B L O C K			LUNCH & RECESS	B L O C K		

EIGHTH GRADE

P	0	1	2	3	4	5	6	7	8	9
BAND & HONORS CHORUS	T A P	B L O C K		EXPL & PE/H	BLOCK	LUNCH & RECESS	BLOCK	EXPL & PE/H	B L O C K	

Figure 10.3 A Typical Middle School Block Schedule.

flexibility for core committee meetings once a week. Often, the school counselor takes a leadership role in planning some of the advisor/advisee period activities by preparing packets of material for the teachers to use during the period. Note that the band period and the advisor/advisee period overlap. This is not the perfect solution to scheduling the music program, but it is a commonly used solution. The rationale for the arrangement is that the band/chorus director traditionally acts as a critical friend to the students, and therefore can serve as the advisor for these students.

The central part of the middle school schedule is the block. Simply stated, a group of students and two or three teaches are assigned together in a block of time. Inside this block, the teacher team and the students plan the learning activities. The schedule within the block can be modified for student grouping needs, curriculum needs, or instructional needs without affecting the remainder of the school. A typical arrangement is to assign a language arts teacher with a social studies teacher for a block, perhaps the morning block shown in Figure 10.3, and assign a mathematics and a science teacher together for the afternoon block. These four core subjects are taught during these two blocks each day. However, the teachers have a lot of flexibility in this block. They may spend more time on one subject one day and less the next day; they may take the students on a field trip; or they may teach some concepts together so that the individual subjects merge into a single topic for the day. While the ratio of teachers to students is about 1:30, there may be three teachers and ninety students in the block or two teachers and sixty students.

This block schedule is structured so that all sixth grade students have the same time schedule, all seventh graders have blocks at the same time, etc. This type of block scheduling is important because the blocks (and overall schedules) of all the grades are different, so that sixth grade students do not interact, to any large extent with the eighth grade students. This type of scheduling reduces many student conflicts. One goal is to develop heterogeneous communities of learners who have a special feeling of community.

The smaller blocks shown on the eighth grade schedule allow for special classes which may need to be offered. This example permits a regular high school algebra class to be taught to the academically talented eighth grade mathematics students during one of these small blocks. When special teachers, facilities, or services are needed to meet the needs of the students, the teachers who meet these needs should be brought into the team meeting with the regular teacher team.

An important part of the middle school schedule is the exploratory/physical education/health period. All sixth grade students are exposed to a number of short courses, such as computers, foreign language, home economics, industrial arts, art, library skills, life skills, or music appreciation. The frequency with which physical education and health are offered depends on state mandates. Typically, these courses of short duration are not graded (satisfactory/unsatisfactory is awarded), and students get a chance to explore different academic areas to see which may be of interest to them for more intensive study in the future. As the students advance to the seventh and eighth grades, the number of courses they can select may be reduced, and the length of time in each one may be increased. By the eighth grade, students may be choosing only two or three courses for the year.

Scheduling of the exploratory subjects is extremely important, because it is during these periods that teacher teams have their group planning time for curriculum integration, to discuss common student concerns, and to hold group parent conferences. This is an integral part of making the schedule and program work. Exploratory specialist teachers should have their own team planning time, or should be worked into the regular team meetings. All special education teachers should be a part of some teacher team. The specialist and exploratory teachers can be rotated into the regular teams on an as-needed basis to plan for special curricular or instructional events. Adequate planning time (at least two hours per week of common planning time per team, in addition to individual preparation time) makes it possible for this type of scheduling to work effectively.

Students are not tracked for achievement in the traditional middle school, but are grouped heterogeneously within the team. They may still be grouped for a short time within the block period in order to meet a short-term instructional goal. Also, there is some selection for students when schools offer courses like algebra in the eighth grade as discussed earlier.

Some other suggestions:

(1) It is important for the school team(s) to develop an identity. Teacher/student teams often select names and slogans which help them have an identity for their particular group.
(2) Discipline should be handled, to a great extent, in advisor/advisee periods. Only more severe cases should go to the office.
(3) As stated earlier, teachers should have the major role in making up

the schedule. Unlike the high school, time does not have to be spent assigning hundreds of students to individual classes, but teachers can easily schedule students within a team.

SCHEDULING THE ELEMENTARY SCHOOL

For people who do not have elementary school experience, the task of scheduling an elementary school might seem very simply—just assign twenty-five to thirty students to a teacher. While this grade assignment does take place, the school schedule is complicated by the special classes that take place in the elementary school. While this section will give suggestions for scheduling, it should be remembered that each school is different. One school may have full-time art, music, and physical education teachers for grades K–6, while another building, housing grades 1–3, may have only part-time teachers in these areas. Schools often must share specialists with other buildings, and therefore travel time must be placed in these teachers' schedules. This arrangement adds another complication to the scheduling. Each building is somewhat unique in the grades contained and in the staff assigned to that school.

Like the other schools discussed earlier, the teachers should be involved in scheduling. It is suggested that a team of teachers work with the principal to schedule the special areas in the elementary school. They can start with the previous year's schedule, and determine if some regular classroom teachers had a perceived advantage that year because of the schedule. For example, if the team feels that it is an advantage to have art or music scheduled later in the day, those teachers who had that arrangement that year had the advantage. To be fair, the team should alternate the schedule from year to year so that any advantage is rotated among all the teachers. The principal should also be aware that a teacher with a dominating personality on the team may unduly influence the other members of the team, perhaps to his/her personal advantage. The principal needs to see that this does not occur.

Another suggestion is to ask teachers to teach reading and mathematics at the same time of day throughout the school. When this is done, there can be grouping across classrooms as well as within classrooms. This scheduling gives flexibility and encourages the teachers to work together creatively for the benefit of individual students. It also encourages articulation within and across the grades. An exercise in elementary scheduling is presented in Figure 10.4.

Other issues which must be considered during scheduling include the

Here is a practice exercise for scheduling an elementary school. Develop a schedule for an elementary school (K – 6) of 567 students with the following breakdown of grade sizes and the number of teachers given below:

Students		Teachers
K	= 64	27 regular classroom
1st	= 76	2 LD resource
2nd	= 80	2 self-contained
3rd	= 63	1 Chapter 1
4th	= 90	1/2 music teacher
5th	= 85	1/2 P.E. teacher
6th	= 92	No art teacher
Spec. Ed.	= 17 (self-contained)	2/5 nurse
		2/5 media specialist
		1/2 computer specialist

***Figure 10.4** Elementary Scheduling Exercise.*

number of special education students, and the need for spaces for those to be included in the regular classes, or space for those who will be mainstreamed on a part-time basis. In addition, if a school has pullout programs for Chapter 1 and/or gifted education, these programs must be considered when developing the schedule in order to reduce conflicts regarding these students and activities such as music and art.

SUMMARY

This chapter detailed the steps for a principal to take to construct a school schedule at the high school, middle school, and elementary school levels, including a discussion of the conflict matrix at the high school.

THE PRINCIPAL'S CASEBOOK

The Case of the Big Board

Dr. Loucks, a newly appointed counselor in a high school of 1,300 students, has just received a copy of the official job description from the superintendent. Under the curriculum area it states that she is responsible for the master schedule of the high school. This had not been discussed during the interview by either the principal or superintendent.

Questions to Consider

- What should she tell the principal?
- What help could she get? From whom?
- Who should she involve in the scheduling process?
- Do *you* feel you have the background to use computer technology or would you schedule by hand?
- Where would you seek information on computer scheduling if the school has not used it in the past?
- What are the advantages and disadvantages of using a computer?

REFERENCE

Jacobson, P. B., W. C. Reavis and J. D. Logsdon. 1963. *The Effective School Principal.* Englewood Cliffs, N.J.: Prentice-Hall, Inc.

One of the authors once had a professor in educational administration who told the class, "I have never seen a good school that didn't also have a good principal. While I have seen bad schools with good principals who just couldn't do enough to get the schools changed, whenever I have seen a good school, there has always been a good principal in the school office."

This professor and research both support the notion that it is essential for a school to have an effective principal if it is to be an effective school. And, as this book described in the beginning, today's school principal has a dual role. To be an effective principal, he/she must be both the instructional leader and the manager of the school. Regardless of the emphasis placed on the instructional role in university courses, the principal will be held accountable for both the instructional and managerial roles.

It is hoped that this book has provided suggestions for becoming more efficient and effective in the managerial role so that principals can find more time to devote to the instructional role in the school. Both roles are legitimate and both are important.

Educational administration often gets ideas from the business world. It is interesting to note that in business, when we discuss a company which has good management, we see this as a very positive aspect. Stockbrokers and mutual fund managers often mention that one of the things they look for in a company is good management. And yet, in educational administration, being thought of as a good manager is almost considered derogatory. One of the authors was once asked at an interview, "Do you consider yourself a leader or a manager?" The "correct" answer was that the administrator was a "leader." To reply that he was a "manager" seemed to place him at a lower level, less important, less skilled. But, the answer should have been, "I consider myself both a leader and a manager. An administrator needs to provide a leadership role in the school, to inspire a vision of what the school can be and, at the same time, the school administrator needs to be a manager of the school, to be sure that it is run efficiently and effectively. Both roles are important if the school is to be a good school. And, I can do both of them!''

*You Can Improve Your School's Image WITHOUT Spending Money**

It has never been more important to have good school-community relations. With open enrollment, choice, and the reluctance of taxpayers to pay more for schools, it is essential that schools examine their public relations efforts and make any necessary changes to improve their programs.

Much has been written about school and district newsletters, annual reports, the use of public relations specialists in the schools, and elaborate brochures about the schools in the district. While all of these have a proper place in the public relations program, they also cost money, and may be beyond the budget of some school districts.

There are, however, important public relations steps that can be taken with a minimum of funds—and only a little time to inservice the staff. These suggestions are very simple and certainly are not new, but they can go a long way toward developing good relationships with the public and the community.

The authors of this article have had the opportunity to visit many schools and to phone many teachers and administrators during the school day. The old saying "You never get a second chance to make a good first impression" certainly rings true in schools today. We found that many of the schools we visited and phoned could have used that second chance, because their first impression was not very good. Here are some suggestions to make a good impression the first time:

Inservice the secretarial staff about how to deal effectively with the public. In almost all cases, the first contact person in a school is a secretary. On the phone, many secretaries appear to want to get rid of callers as soon as possible, saying, "Mr. Jones is not in his office. What is your number, and I'll have him call you back." (Mr. Jones must have

*By William L. Sharp, James K. Walter, and Helen M. Sharp.

stacks of call slips on his desk.) Secretaries need to demonstrate a helpful attitude that shows they care about the caller and his/her concerns. A simple, "Thank you for calling Maple High School. May I help you?" would be a good start. A good secretary should be able to offer help beyond taking phone numbers.

Use adults to answer all incoming phone calls. Many schools use students to help answer the phone. Because we have been administrators, we know why this is done. Yet, it is disconcerting to phone a school, get a student on the line, and realize that you cannot make her understand the purpose of your call. Again, the caller ends up resorting to leaving a phone number. One time, one of us called for an elementary principal, and the student (fifth or sixth grade student) ran all the way out to the playground to get the principal before we could stop her. No business would consider using an eleven-year-old to be its first contact with the public. Schools do it all the time. Put the students to other uses in the school office, or use them to show visitors around the building. Let the secretary answer the phone, please.

Provide visible and clear directions to the main office. When visiting, we usually encounter the standard sign on the door: *All Visitors Must Report to the Office.* (And, in today's times, we find almost all the doors locked, too, but we understand the need for that.) Once we find an unlocked door and enter, there is not a clue as to where the office is located. No matter how large or small the building, a good locator map showing your position (and the office) would be very helpful to those with first-time business in the school.

Train the secretaries to greet visitors once they arrive at the school office. Once the office is found, we often found a student behind the office counter. She was usually discussing the ball game or dance with another student who was late for class (and becoming later). Unfortunately, we found that the secretaries are often not much better. With some exceptions, they were often drinking coffee, having a snack, and talking to other people. A secretary needs to be trained to greet strangers warmly, ask their business ("May I help you?"), perhaps offer them a cup of coffee, and ask them to be seated while they find the answer or locate the person needed by the visitor.

Advise secretaries to warn the principal or administrator of special situations or potential problems. If the school visitor seems upset (like a parent bringing the principal a problem), the secretary needs to warn the principal. We recall one principal turning a negative situation into a positive one by merely saying, "You look like you could use a cup of coffee. May I get you one before we talk?" This gesture showed concern, and it allowed the parent to cool off so that the meeting with the principal became a discussion instead of a confrontation.

Encourage your staff (teachers, especially) and students to notice visitors entering the building, and to ask them if they need directions. This is not only good public relations, it makes the school a little bit safer, too.

Besides these suggestions dealing with those who phone or visit the school, here are some additional suggestions to improve public relations with parents.

Review the importance of positive parent communications with the faculty. Devote some faculty meeting or inservice time to review positive telephone and written communications with teachers. Make sure they understand the important opportunity for positive public relations conveyed by voice tone, the message, suggestions for parents and students and call-backs.

You might introduce discussion of positive written communications with this example of a negative note or one like it. This is the opening line of an actual midsemester deficiency report (which might be the only contact these parents had with the school during the semester in which it was sent): "This is a follow-up to the forgery incident."

Teachers understand specifics. Note the positive impact of these alternate approaches. "Karen's regular attendance is the key to her success in math," or "Scott's overall ability is not reflected in his current grade average," or "Brenda might benefit from individual help, and I'm in the building for an hour before and after school four days a week," or "Can I enlist your help with Janice's attention to her own work during reading sessions?"

Feature student efforts in district newsletters. These need not be whole essays, but try to include journal excerpts, short poems, drawings, slogans or captions, contest entries, etc., that show parents how students are succeeding.

Offer any interested parents the opportunity to meet informally with school administrators and/or board members once or twice monthly—mornings and/or evenings. One school district used a second-cup-of-coffee format in morning meetings with district parents and community members. Course goals, new programs, test scores, and a wide range of topics can be discussed—whatever concerns parents and adults.

Submit news releases about student efforts and achievements to local newspapers on a monthly basis. Enlist the aid of journalism classes or newspaper staff members to write newspaper-ready features on all aspects of student effort in the district. Regular reminders via local newspapers tell parents about what is going right in schools.

Send home only positively worded notices and communications, and revise any that create a negative or even a neutral impression. An administrator-teacher committee should periodically review routine correspondence sent home to parents. Whatever is written about your schools or its students can be both informative and positive.

Set up a vehicle for offering positive suggestions, whether a special phone extension or postcard mailing. Improving the image of the school is everyone's responsibility. Make good school public relations a district goal. Accept suggestions from parents and teachers; many times they notice what administrators may overlook.

Reach into the community and draw on the expertise available. Always include parents and community members in special activities, including art fairs, district contests, special assemblies, minicourses, skill days, activity periods, etc. Make your school the focus of student-adult interaction in meaningful, planned programs that bring community specialists into your school.

Whatever is written, maintain the commitment to successful public relations as a district goal. Administrators in particular need to be aware of successful writing strategies that create positive, favorable impressions no matter what the situation. Public relations experts and business people know how to reach their public, and business writing texts offer schools a unique perspective on the techniques of successfully relaying messages. Raymond V. Lesikar's *Basic Business Communication* (Homewood, IL: Richard D. Irvin, Inc., 1988) includes some of the following helpful tips:

(1) Use the objective tone.
(2) Write factual messages, including specifics wherever necessary.
(3) Emphasize nouns and verbs stand out and draw reader attention (adjectives and adverbs delay or break vital messages).
(4) Write short paragraphs (two to four sentences each).
(5) Revise sentences with careful word choice to effectively convey just the right meaning.

(6) Adapt wording to an audience (in our case, no "educationese").
(7) Use topic sentences for paragraphs so that the main idea is immediately evident.
(8) Make ideas progress logically in a letter or communication.
(9) Feature only one idea per sentence and one idea per paragraph.
(10) Keep sentences to a maximum of eighteen words.
(11) Strive for the good will effect (anything that focuses on benefits or courtesy).
(12) Highlight the beginnings and endings of sentences and paragraphs with key ideas (these are points of emphasis in any communication).
(13) Use list forms, with numbers, bullets, dashes, etc., whenever possible.
(14) Repeat and isolate the most important points in a message or communication.
(15) Always convey a positive rather than a negative impression (keep your audience in mind and how they are likely to react).

Building and maintaining good school-community relations is a goal for many school districts. There are steps that can be taken to welcome visitors or callers, to keep the public informed about school activities and to create positive favorable impressions with parents and the community. The starting point seems to be the recognition of deficiencies and a commitment to improve. Using the steps described above, any district can begin to change the features that are less than satisfactory and/or improve school-home communications and the school's image. It's not a question of money, but taking the time to analyze and plan new strategies.

Detention and School Rules

The following rules are suggested for after school detention (ASD). They can also be adapted for use for inside suspension.

(1) There is to be no talking at any time during ASD.

(2) Students are not permitted to leave the ASD room. Restroom use and necessary books and materials should be taken care of before coming to ASD.

(3) There is to be no eating or gum chewing during ASD.

(4) Students are to stay in their seats until ASD is over, facing the front of the classroom—no turning around.

(5) Tardiness of any kind will not be tolerated.

(6) There is to be no writing on blackboards, working of school equipment, or disturbing the bulletin boards.

(7) Students must have writing equipment before ASD starts. The pencil sharpener cannot be used once ASD begins.

(8) Sleeping, misconduct, or not studying can result in additional day(s) of assignment or out-of-school suspension.

(9) If a student is absent while serving ASD, even if it is excused, the student must make the time up. A student cannot be excused from ASD.

(10) Students in ASD cannot socialize with students who are not assigned to ASD.

(11) Students cannot leave the ASD room until dismissed by the person supervising the room.

(12) Any problems in the ASD room will be reported by the supervisor to the principal.

Some of the incidents that typically might lead to a detention are the following:

Date________________

Dear_____________________.
This note is to inform you that your son/daughter, _______________, will be staying after school for detention on_______________. The length of detention will be __________ minutes for__________ days, or from 2:45 PM until _____ ______________.

This after-school detention has been assigned by the administration because the teacher has done everything possible to correct the student in the classroom. We hope that this will take care of the problem, and that your child will be able to behave properly in the future.

Should after-school detention not work, or should your child fail to report, the next alternative may be suspension from school.

We are informing you in advance so that you can make arrangements for your child's transportation on the day(s) of detention. We also hope that you will discuss this with your child so that the problem will not happen in the future. Thank you for your cooperation.

____
Principal

***Figure B.1** Sample ASD Letter.*

Student Name ______________________Grade _________________________
Nature of Offense ____
____
____

Name of Teacher ____
What Subject(s) Student Is to Work on ___________________________
____
____
____

Name of Assigning Administrator _________________________________
Amount of Detention Time Each Day ______________________________
Day(s) Assigned Detention ______________________________________
____

Name of Detention Supervisor ___________________________________
Did Student Report? Yes__________ No__________
Supervisor Comments (if any) ___________________________________
____
____

For this form, the teacher completes the first third, the administrator the middle, and the ASD supervisor the last part.

***Figure B.2** ASD Recommendation Form.*

- lessons poorly prepared or not done at all
- inattention in class
- bad language
- a poor attitude in class
- tardiness in coming to school or to the classroom
- frequent absences
- cutting classes
- smoking
- disrespect to an adult staff member
- disruptive behavior anywhere on school grounds
- other violations deemed appropriate by the administration

Figure B.1 is a sample letter which can be used to inform parents of an after-school detention, assuming the school ends at 2:45 PM (A more formal letter should be used for an actual suspension.

Figure B.2 is a form which teachers can use to recommend the assignment of detention.

Some of the forms and guidelines have been adapted from those used at Maple Crest School, Kokomo, Indiana.

Information Management Software

Today, there are several good vendors with computer software which can be used to help school principals do some of their managerial tasks. The authors asked Karen L. Hartle, the marketing communications coordinator for National Computer Systems (NCS), to provide some information on the types of software available from NCS which might be helpful to principals. This appendix, written by Ms. Hartle and NCS, is the response to our request.

It is often said that we must practice what we preach. Lead by example. This is because kids do as adults do, not necessarily as they say. As we enter deeper and deeper into the information age, we feel compelled to teach our students how to become masters of technology and, subsequently, information. Educators are beginning to realize how critical it is that they find the means to become masters of information and technology themselves. Many are finding that the allocation of precious time and financial resources is an investment that proves rewarding in many ways. After all, how can we teach our students to thrive in an information age if we do not master it ourselves?

Mastering information in the 90s requires proficiency with hardware, software, and data collection tools, along with the dedication of the people managing a school's administration. This Appendix will give examples of tools some schools have used to master information.

National Computer Systems developed a comprehensive system of computer software for schools in 1985. This system, called CIMS™III (Comprehesive Information Management for Schools), was marketed by IBM and is used by more than 4,500 districts nationwide.

Many principals are familiar with NCS scannable forms which are used with optical mark reading scanners for testing. Similar technology can be used on a broader scale as well. The miracle of automation has ventured beyond testing to class scheduling, attendance taking, grading, and survey/evaluation processing. In fact, automation is now often used for smaller-scale management of information for such things as discipline tracking and vehicle registration. Data can be entered automatically and processed into valuable information available in various formats within minutes. Following are several examples of the use of computer technology which can help the school principal.

MASTER SCHEDULING TECHNOLOGY FOR THE 21ST CENTURY

Technology has advanced to the point where automation can accommodate a variety of scheduling formats, including: conventional, modular, mosaic, block, and selective exploration. Automatic schedule generation, on-line drop/add features, and extensive reporting capabilities are also available. A flexible, leading-edge system will allow mass changes to be made to the schedule based on specific criteria such as grade level, gender, course, and section. A good system will also enable variation of the full-time-equivalency value for each course section.

AUTOMATED ATTENDANCE TAKING

Entry and management of individual student and staff attendance has come a long way in the last decade. With an automated system, daily attendance information no longer takes hours to process. It can be processed accurately, literally within minutes. State and federal ADA and ADM reporting information can be generated at the touch of a key, rather than taking days to calculate and verify. Most importantly, schools may be able to obtain more state funding if they have software that can prove the validity of absences in special circumstances.

One of the biggest benefits of an automated attendance system is that it enhances the communication link between educators and parents. Parents can be notified instantly when a child is not in school on a given day. In addition to the public relations benefit, most states require that a parent or guardian be notified if a child is absent without being excused. Automatic phone dialing systems are now available to call parents, and to track and print reports on who was contacted, the response, date, and time called. These systems can even leave messages for parents on answering machines. Finally, the autodialer can then report that it has left a message. As one elementary principal in Arizona observed, "Not only do we have machines talking to machines, but we have machines telling us they've talked to machines."

TEST AUTOMATION

Automatic testing has become a controversial topic over the past few years. With the increasing emphasis on portfolio assessment, some educators avoid multiple-choice tests at all costs. However, multiple-choice tests, when used in conjunction with essay-style questions, can be a very effective way of measuring students against predetermined standards.

Multiple-choice testing has become more sophisticated. For example, a test question might ask students for an answer from *A* to *F* and then ask the students how *certain* they are of that answer (*1* being "Not Very Certain" and *5* being "Extremely Certain.") Then, if a student selects *A* as correct and that student is "Extremely Certain.") the student might receive 10 points. If the same student selects *A* and "Somewhat Certain," the student only receives 8 points. On the other hand, if the student selects the wrong answer and realizes and admits that he/she was not sure of the answer, that student will not have as many points deducted as the student that selects the wrong answer and insists that it is correct.

In order to meet the changing needs in the area of educational assessment, some computer companies (including NCS) have developed innovative ways to automate the evaluation of performance-based assessments. This can be done by a process known as image scanning. This process greatly assists educators with the portfolio style of assessment.

USING COMPUTERS FOR GRADING

Accurate and precise grading can be one of the best ways to spare a lot of agony and suffering. Using an automated system for grading can be one of the best ways to obtain accurate grades.

Flexibility is probably the single most important factor to consider when selecting an automated grade reporting system. A system that allows user-defined alpha, numeric, or short-word grades, and that accepts data from both keyboards and scanners, is likely to offer the principal the most comprehensive solution. Top-of-the-line systems even allow for weekly distributions of reports for students at risk of poor grades. Comprehensive systems allow for user definition of items such as excessive absences influencing class/course credit. Report writing capabilities are also important to consider. While the initial investment may be higher for these systems, savings may result in the long run.

AUTOMATED SURVEYS AND EVALUATIONS

In an increasingly customer-service oriented society, surveys, and evaluations are critical to the survival of any organization. The education industry is no exception. Schools can purchase generic scannable forms and actually overprint survey questions onto those forms, then scan and tally them in-house. This allows for localized control, which means ease of preparation and fast turnaround of results. Thus, the process of improvement can occur more rapidly. This is something that makes any school really shine.

AUTOMATED DISCIPLINE TRACKING

Discipline is one of the more complicated areas associated with the job of the principal. To keep from complicating it further, it is a good idea to try to automate disciplinary information as much as possible. That way, when a student's parent calls up to question why that student was punished, the principal will be able to look it up on the computer system instantly, and check on those details that might be needed to validate the administration's position on the matter.

A CASE HISTORY

The following case history illustrates how one school district made decisions to use technology to manage its information.

In the early 1990s, several employees of a Phoenix, Arizona, district formed a committee to pool all the technology information they had as individuals, and come up with information management solutions tailor-made for their district.

After the committee had begun their work, the school administration brought in technology experts to share their knowledge with the committee and to work with them to form solutions. The district became a pilot district for hardware (IBM) and software (NCS). The CIMS™III, mentioned earlier, was initially used to manage student demographics and registration. By 1992, it was also used to streamline attendance, grading, and scheduling.

In order to determine how to make the best use of the new products, a group of teachers, school and district office staff, state department education staff, and vendors began meeting every two weeks. The meeting became a forum to share problems, develop solutions, and assign responsibilities. The administration stated that this committee "was what got the pilot up and functioning, which ultimately led to our success with data and information management."

Their creativity paid off. Knowing, of course, that no software program had been created especially for their district, they worked with the various programs they had in order to develop solutions for their district.

At one point, they started to look for a way to develop reports that would cross-reference data, showing how different elements, such as attendance, affect other elements, such as achievement scores. New state requirements were asking for this type of information. In most districts, educators do not have the ability to cross-reference these databases to see how students are doing. This district hopes to see if there are relationships between the different variables in the databases.

The more the district looked into the capabilities of their software system, the more they realized what could be done. For example, while the state might have ten criteria for measuring a student's success, the district may have twelve, and the teacher could have as many as fourteen. There is enough flexibility with the software to track all the criteria, and the committee was able to learn how it could be done, enhancing their knowledge for future applications.

The software is used to create a variety of reports showing the progress of specific groups of students, as well as recording alternative types of assessment. These reports could include portfolio assessment, which looks at observable behavior that cannot be tested in a traditional manner.

The district has found that adding technology improves the learning process by freeing up students and teachers from tasks, and giving them more time to work on thinking skills. Teachers are able to access specific student or classroom information easily, without sorting through a maze of unrelated information.

Attendance is taken on-line using the CIMS™III software. The data is processed as it enters the system, and attendance information can be processed immediately. An automatic dialing system contacts the parents of the absent children.

The reaction from parents has been very positive. One parent enrolled her child in the school after seeing what was happening, while another parent loaned thirty-two PCs to the district for two years, until the district could fund an additional computer lab itself. This latter parent did this after her child developed a greater interest in learning after being introduced to computers.

This district has a mission to provide the very best educational opportunities to its students in the year 2000 and beyond, and it felt that the use of technology was crucial in order to make that happen.

FURTHER SUGGESTIONS

Other districts which may wish to use technology in a similar way should heed these suggestions:

- Look at different technological options.
- When examining a vendor, be sure it can offer a comprehensive solution to the district's information management needs.
- Establish a business partnership with a technology company large enough to respond to the district's needs.
- Each district has specialized needs. Be sure the company can respond to those needs, not just offer a generic program.
- Look for a company that has experience in technology, and one which has shown that it can change as technology changes and as the district information management needs change.

INDEX

Dr. William L. Sharp is an Associate Professor in the Department of Educational Administration and Higher Education and Associate Dean of the College of Education at Southern Illinois University at Carbondale. Prior to this position, he held a similar position at the University of Akron, and was a school superintendent in Indiana and Illinois before his university positions. During his superintendencies, *Executive Educator* selected him as one of the top 100 superintendents in the country. He has an A.B. in mathematics and an M.S. in secondary education from Indiana University, a graduate diploma from Durham University in England, where he was a Durham Scholar, and a Ph.D. from Northwestern University. He has had articles published in numerous education journals, *The New York Times,* and the *Cleveland Plain Dealer.* His first book, *Collective Bargaining in the Public Schools,* was published by Brown and Benchmark. His wife, Helen, also writes extensively about education and English.

Dr. James K. Walter is superintendent of Dudley Charlton Regional School District in Massachusetts, and is also president of James K. Walter and Associates, an educational consulting and school executive search firm he founded in 1988. Prior to his superintendency, Dr. Walter was an assistant professor of educational administration at the University of Akron, and an adjunct professor at Ashland University, Ohio, and at Indiana University. A native of Kokomo, Indiana, he received his B.S. in English education from Indiana University and his M.A.E. and Ed.D. in school administration and curriculum from Ball State University. Dr. Walter brings a wealth of experience as a teacher and administrator at all levels of public school administration, and is the author of numerous articles and essays for professional books and journals. He is the author of the Phi Delta Kappa booklet, *The Elementary Principal as Fiscal Manager.* He and his wife Deborah, an X-ray technician, have two children, Zachary and Andrea.